Microsoft Mapping

Geospatial Development with Bing Maps and C#

Ray Rischpater
Carmen Au

Apress·

Microsoft Mapping: Geospatial Development with Bing Maps and C#

ISBN-13 (pbk): 978-1-4302-6109-4

ISBN-13 (electronic): 978-1-4302-6110-0

President and Publisher: Paul Manning
Lead Editor: Ewan Buckingham
Technical Reviewer: Fabio Claudio Ferracchiati
Editorial Board: Steve Anglin, Mark Beckner, Ewan Buckingham, Gary Cornell, Louise Corrigan, Jonathan Gennick, Jonathan Hassell, Robert Hutchinson, Michelle Lowman, James Markham, Matthew Moodie, Jeff Olson, Jeffrey Pepper, Douglas Pundick, Ben Renow-Clarke, Dominic Shakeshaft, Gwenan Spearing, Matt Wade, Steve Weiss, Tom Welsh, James T. DeWolf
Coordinating Editor: Christine Ricketts
Copy Editor: Lori Cavanaugh
Compositor: SPi Global
Indexer: SPi Global
Artist: SPi Global
Cover Designer: Anna Ishchenko

Distributed to the book trade worldwide by Springer Science+Business Media New York, 233 Spring Street, 6th Floor, New York, NY 10013. Phone 1-800-SPRINGER, fax (201) 348-4505, e-mail orders-ny@springer-sbm.com, or visit www.springeronline.com. Apress Media, LLC is a California LLC and the sole member (owner) is Springer Science + Business Media Finance Inc (SSBM Finance Inc). SSBM Finance Inc is a Delaware corporation.

For information on translations, please e-mail rights@apress.com, or visit www.apress.com.

Apress and friends of ED books may be purchased in bulk for academic, corporate, or promotional use. eBook versions and licenses are also available for most titles. For more information, reference our Special Bulk Sales–eBook Licensing web page at www.apress.com/bulk-sales.

Any source code or other supplementary materials referenced by the author in this text is available to readers at www.apress.com. For detailed information about how to locate your book's source code, go to www.apress.com/source-code/.

In memory of Meredith and Raymond White, with copious gratitude for years of the maps in National Geographic.

—Ray

This book is dedicated to my dad, David, for inspiring me to become an engineer, to my mom, Oymoon, for being my greatest teacher, to my sister, Melanie, for always looking out for me, and to my husband, Elijah, for always enthusiastically supporting my crazy ideas, like writing a textbook in my spare time.

—Carmen

Contents at a Glance

About the Authors..xi

About the Technical Reviewer xiii

Acknowledgments xv

Introduction xvii

■Chapter 1: Getting Started with Microsoft and Mapping...1

■Chapter 2: Painless Hosting with Azure 11

■Chapter 3: Geospatial with Azure SQL Database 29

■Chapter 4: Hosting WCF Services on Windows Azure..47

■Chapter 5: Map Visualization with Bing Maps for the Web 65

■Chapter 6: Doing More with Bing Maps 79

■Chapter 7: Bing Maps for WPF...101

■Chapter 8: Bing Maps for Windows Store Apps...117

■Chapter 9: Bing Maps for Windows Phone 8 135

■Chapter 10: Power Map for Excel 147

Index...155

Contents

About the Authors..xi

About the Technical Reviewer xiii

Acknowledgments xv

Introduction xvii

■Chapter 1: Getting Started with Microsoft and Mapping..1

Mapping and Microsoft 1

    Bing Maps for Developers 2

    Microsoft SQL Server for Location Applications 3

    Windows Azure to Host Your Application 3

    Maps Without Code: Power Maps 4

What You Need to Get Started 4

A Few Words on Terminology 4

Introducing the Sample Application 6

Developing Your Application 9

Wrapping Up...10

■Chapter 2: Painless Hosting with Azure 11

Why Windows Azure? 11

    Cloud Computing Services..11

    Windows Azure Data Management..13

Setting up Windows Azure...15

    Getting a Windows Azure Account 15

    Getting the Windows Azure SDK 17

Hosting a Bing Map on Azure 18

    Obtaining a Bing Maps Account 18

    Obtaining a Bing Maps Key 18

    Building the Bing Map 19

    Hosting the Bing Map on Windows Azure 21

Wrapping Up 27

■Chapter 3: Geospatial with Azure SQL Database 29

SQL Database Overview 29

    Accessing Data in SQL Database 29

    SQL Database Architecture.Overview 30

    SQL Database Provisioning Model 32

    Federations in SQL Database 33

Geospatial representation in SQL Database 34

    Spatial Reference Systems Overview 34

    SQL Database Spatial Data Types 34

Setting up a SQL Database 36

Inserting geospatial data into a SQL Database 41

Wrapping up 46

■Chapter 4: Hosting WCF Services on Windows Azure 47

WCF: A Crash Course 47

    Services 47

    Endpoints 48

    WCF Client 51

WCF Service for Earthquake Data 52

    Creating the WCF Service 52

    Hosting the WCF Service on Azure 58

    Client Application 61

Wrapping Up 64

■Chapter 5: Map Visualization with Bing Maps for the Web 65

Bing Maps Ajax Control Basics..65

Map Markers 68

Polygons 71

Putting it all together...73

Create the Model 73

Loading the Earthquake Data (The Controller)..75

Displaying the Earthquake Data (The View)..75

Wrapping Up 78

■Chapter 6: Doing More with Bing Maps...79

Location..79

Where is it?...80

Where am I? 84

Routing 86

Sample Routing Query Application 86

Directions Module...89

Traffic 93

Theming 96

Building Your Own Modules...98

Wrapping Up 100

■Chapter 7: Bing Maps for WPF...101

Introducing the Bing Maps for WPF Control 101

Getting the Control 102

Key Classes and Relationships..102

Using the Control 104

Kicking the Tires 104

Earthquakes Everywhere!...108

Geocoding with the Bing Maps Geocoder Service...112

Routing with the Bing Maps Routing Service 113

Wrapping Up 116

Chapter 8: Bing Maps for Windows Store Apps 117

Introducing Bing Maps for Windows Store 117

Seeing the Bing.Maps Map Control in Action 120

    Your First Windows Store Map App...120

    Interacting with Landmarks and Venues 121

    Creating a Custom Pushpin 123

    Extra Credit: Finding Yourself on the Map 126

    Putting it All Together The Earthquake App 129

Wrapping Up 134

Chapter 9: Bing Maps for Windows Phone 8 135

Introducing Bing Maps for Windows Phone 8...135

Getting Started With Bing Maps for Windows Phone 8 137

Finding Yourself on the Map 138

Putting it All Together: The Earthquake App 140

Wrapping Up 145

Chapter 10: Power Map for Excel 147

Introducing Power Map 147

Getting Started with Power Map 148

    Navigating around Power Map 149

    Map Options in Power Map...150

    Configuring the Presentation of a Layer 151

    Styling the Power Map Result 152

Wrapping Up 153

Index...155

About the Authors

Ray Rischpater is an engineer and author with over twenty years of experience writing about and developing software for mobile and Internet platforms.

During this time, he's participated in the development of Internet technologies and custom applications for Microsoft Windows, Java ME, Qualcomm BREW, Apple iPhone, Google Android, Palm OS, Apple Newton, and Magic Cap. Presently, he's employed as a senior scientist at Microsoft building 3D maps.

When not writing for or about mobile platforms, he enjoys amateur radio with the call sign KF6GPE, hiking, and photography with his family and friends in and around the San Lorenzo Valley in central California.

Carmen Au is a Scientist at Microsoft and works on building 3D maps. Before joining Microsoft, she worked in a research lab developing visual navigation mobile device applications. Her work in map navigation has been published in various academic conferences and journals, and has been patented and featured in *New Scientist* magazine and on the CBS News website. Carmen received her B.Eng, M.Eng, and Ph.D. in Computer Engineering at McGill University, her doctoral work in Computer Vision and Augmented Reality. Born and raised in Montreal, Canada, she moved to the Silicon Valley in 2011. In her spare time, Carmen sits on the Sunnyvale Board of Chamber of Commerce, travels, enjoys cooking, and attends classical music concerts with her husband.

About the Technical Reviewer

Fabio Claudio Ferracchiati is a senior consultant and a senior analyst/developer using Microsoft technologies. He works for Brain Force (`www.brainforce.com`) in its Italian branch (`www.brainforce.it`). He is a Microsoft Certified Solution Developer for .NET, a Microsoft Certified Application Developer for .NET, a Microsoft Certified Professional, and a prolific author and technical reviewer. Over the past ten years, he's written articles for Italian and international magazines and coauthored more than ten books on a variety of computer topics.

Acknowledgments

It never ceases to amaze us how much writing a book is really a team effort, and in the scheme of things, how much is done by people other than the authors. Yet it's always the authors that get front billing on the cover. It doesn't seem fair.

At Apress, we need to thank Ewan Buckingham and Christine Ricketts for working with our original proposal and shepherding the manuscript through all of its phases. Of course, there are others at Apress who play important roles, too; thanks to Lori Cavanaugh for copyediting, and Anna Ishchenko for the cover design, as well as all of those we don't get to work with personally responsible for the process of making sure that getting books into your hands is a process you can make a business of.

We really appreciate Fabio Claudio Ferracchiati for his feedback throughout the process as our technical reviewer. It's amazingly easy to mis-copy something from Visual Studio into Microsoft Word, even with cut and paste; Fabio caught those kinds of errors, as well as some peskier ones that crept in. Of course, any mistakes that remain are our own.

We must also thank our teammates at Microsoft: while this was a personal project of ours done on our own time, our peers gave us the encouragement to work on the project, as well as opportunities to learn what we're showing you in this book as well as show them what we learned writing this book for you.

Finally, we must thank our families for their patience as we spent time with our computers instead of them on the weekends and evenings that were our time to bring this book to you.

Introduction

From the early days of mapping and road directions on the web to today's proliferation of ubiquitous maps, location-aware recommendation and social applications, and vertical applications for nearly every sector, the last decade has seen an explosion in location-aware software and services.

We're excited to share Microsoft's map-enabling technologies with you. As we show you in Chapter 1, Microsoft is no newcomer to mapping the world; its efforts date back over a decade. Today, Microsoft offers map controls for its leading platforms—Windows Phone, Windows 7, Windows 8, and the Web using HTML and AJAX—as well as enabling geospatial data in its SQL Server and SQL Azure offerings. In addition, the base platform provided by .NET, Windows Communication Foundation (WCF), and Windows Azure gives you a robust hosting solution on which to build and deploy Web and networked applications.

This book gives you the essential information you need to know to use these technologies to build your first location-aware application on any one of Microsoft's platforms; or several of them. While not an in-depth reference on either Windows Azure or WCF, we show you what you need to get started with Windows Azure and SQL Azure to host your application, and WCF to provide the communications backbone between your application clients and your server back end. Then we cover each of Microsoft's map controls in detail, so you can learn how to craft your application for Windows 7, Windows 8, Windows Phone, or the web. Along the way, we provide references to other books and the web, so you can get more detail on the subjects that interest you the most.

We wrote this book for developers with some broad experience using ASP, C#, and .NET, but don't expect you to be deeply proficient in the subject matter. Some experience with the Extensible Application Markup Language (XAML) helps, too, because of course it's the foundation for creating GUIs using Windows Presentation Foundation (WPF) and for writing applications for Windows Store on Windows 8 and Windows 8.1.

We think that Microsoft offers the only soup-to-nuts solution for building location-aware applications, from hosting to presentation, along with the tools to support the platforms you use. We look forward to seeing what applications you create!

CHAPTER 1

Getting Started with Microsoft and Mapping

Location and mapping play an increasingly important role in software today. The advent of location-aware social applications, web sites like Bing Maps, Google Maps, and Yelp, mobile mapping and navigation applications, and location-aware games like Shadow Cities by Grey Area have all increased customer demand for software that knows, presents, and uses your location in helpful ways.

Building these applications from scratch is not easy—in addition to the usual problems of scaling and software development in general, location-aware applications pose additional problems in the area of content (such as the underlying map, points of interest, traffic, and routing), and the back-end storage necessary to quickly index, store, and search data by its position on the earth. Open-source solutions exist; many database vendors have SQL extensions for storing data such as latitude and longitude, and there are user interface controls for a number of platforms, such as Google Maps for the Web and controls on Android and iOS. Only Microsoft, however, provides a soup-to-nuts solution for writing location-aware applications including:

- Microsoft SQL Server, which provides support for geospatial types and operations,

- Windows Azure, which provides platform-as-a-service (PaaS) and infrastructure-as-a-service (IaaS) solutions for hosting your application's services,

- Bing Maps controls for presenting maps with your data on the web and in native applications on Windows and iOS,

- Services provided for traffic and routing overlaid on Bing Maps controls.

In this chapter, we introduce what Microsoft offers to you and how this book is organized. After reading this chapter, you'll have a good understanding of how Microsoft technologies can help you build your location-aware application, how this book is organized, and where to turn next to learn the gritty details you need to build your application.

Mapping and Microsoft

Microsoft has a long history in providing software for mapping, starting with Microsoft MapPoint (first launched in 2000) and TerraServer, a collaboration between Microsoft Research (MSR) and the United States Geological Service (USGS) in continuous operation from 1998 through May of 2012, as well as the various iterations of Web-based mapping solutions culminating in Bing Maps. In addition to making map data available in commercial software and online, Microsoft also makes its map control available for Windows, permitting native application developers access to the same visual presentation as Microsoft provides on its Web sites. In addition, Microsoft has provided significant back-end support for applications that use location and map data, starting with support for geospatial data types introduced in Microsoft SQL Server 2008 with continued support in releases through the present day. More recently, Microsoft has made these features of Microsoft SQL Server available as part of the SQL Database service on Windows Azure, Microsoft's cloud computing service. Let's take a closer look at the capabilities Microsoft provides.

Bing Maps for Developers

You may already be familiar with Bing Maps on the web, especially if you use Bing when you search for points of interest like restaurants and businesses. Although not as widely adopted in mash-ups and other applications as Google Maps, Bing Maps has a developer API comparable with Google Maps, letting you develop asynchronous JavaScript and XML (AJAX) applications for the Web. This AJAX API lets web developers build map-aware applications that can:

- Display street and aerial maps of any region, letting the user zoom and pan the map presented,

- Annotate a displayed map with markers, lines, and regions organized in overlays, letting you add your data to the map,

- Plot directions and traffic information provided by Bing Maps,

- Obtain indoor venue maps for many shopping districts and indoor venues,

- Geocode (determine the latitude and longitude for an address), and reverse geocode (determine an address for a latitude and longitude) to refine your user experience, and

- Search for businesses using Bing.

In addition to making a Web control available, Microsoft makes an embeddable map control available with similar features. This map control, which you can see in Figure 1-1, supports most of the same features as the AJAX version and is available for Windows 8 (Windows Store) applications, as well as for Windows Presentation Foundation (WPF), Windows Phone, and Apple iOS.

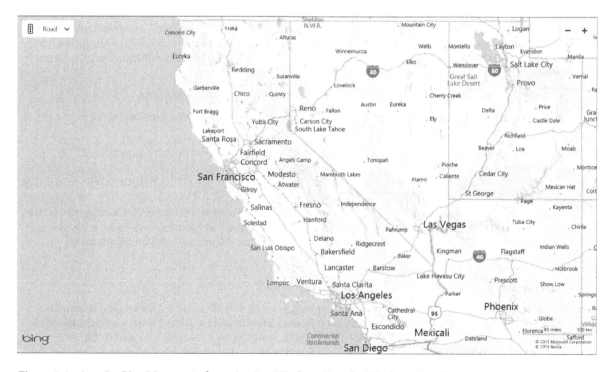

Figure 1-1. *A native Bing Maps control running in a Windows Store for Windows 8 application*

Learning how to use the various flavors of the Bing Maps control is a key part of this book, and we spend a lot of time discussing the various features available to you in the various flavors Microsoft offers. For more information about the control, see Chapters 5 and 6 (where we discuss the Web flavor of the control), Chapters 7 and 8 (where we discuss the Windows 8 and WPF versions of the control, respectively), and Chapter 9 (where we discuss using the control in Windows Phone applications).

Microsoft SQL Server for Location Applications

A growing number of databases support extensions for geospatial applications, and Microsoft SQL Server is no exception. In Microsoft SQL Server 2008, Microsoft introduced data types for both round-earth and planar (projective) mapping. In addition to data types to store geospatial data, Microsoft added support for Simple Feature Access (ISO 19125) support for two-dimensional geographic data, including approximately 70 methods from the specification. In 2012, with Microsoft SQL Server 2012, Microsoft significantly extended this support, adding new methods and new types of geometry for specific applications.

With its spatial extensions in Microsoft SQL Server, you can:

- Store points, lines, polygons, and other shapes in a flat coordinate system using the geometry spatial data type.

- Store points, lines, polygons, and other shapes in a round-earth coordinate system using the geography data type.

- Perform computations on collections of points, such as computing a polygon's area or perimeter, determining if a point falls inside or outside a region, and determining the intersection between regions.

- Build spatial indices over spatial data, letting you perform database searches by location quickly over thousands or millions of points.

You have access to Microsoft SQL Server's location-based features both if you're running stand-alone instances of Microsoft SQL Server as well as in the SQL Database Service on Windows Azure if you choose to host your application on Windows Azure.

We provide a gentle introduction to storing geospatial data using Microsoft SQL Server in Chapter 3. For a more thorough treatment for those with professional database experience, we recommend you check out a copy of *Pro Spatial with SQL Server 2012* by Alistair Aitchison, also from Apress.

Windows Azure to Host Your Application

Most applications today require a back-end component to host data and services. Whether you're building a Web application or just the back-end services to support a client application, Windows Azure gives you a platform to deploy your services.

Windows Azure is more than just a hosting service; it provides scalable infrastructure for deploying your services that includes:

- Easy partitioning into storage, web, and worker hosts running Windows Server in one or more geographic regions for redundancy,

- Relational storage through the SQL Database Service,

- NoSQL table storage through key-value pairs, as well as the storage of blobs and smaller data blocks (ideal for inter-host communication and processing) through queues,

- • Inter-host messaging through the Windows Azure Service Bus,

- • Support for Microsoft's web hosting through Microsoft Internet Information Services (IIS), letting you serve static as well as dynamic content through Active Server Pages (ASP) with ASP. NET and ASP Model-View-Controller (MVC) (or, if you prefer, PHP or Node.js).

In this book, we discuss Windows Azure as it pertains to hosting location-aware applications in the cloud, especially as a host for running the SQL Database Service and Microsoft IIS. In Chapter 2, you'll get started with your own trial Azure account and deploy a simple Bing Maps application for the web; in Chapters 3 and 4 you learn how to configure the SQL Database Service to store data for your application and construct Windows Communication Foundation (WCF) endpoints for your Web and native client applications. If that's not enough about Windows Azure, for you, we recommend *Windows Azure Platform* by Tejaswi Redkar and Tony Guidici, also from Apress.

Maps Without Code: Power Maps

Sometimes you just need to visualize a data set on a map, either as part of developing a larger solution or just to examine a particular data set. While you can write custom data visualization code using the Bing Maps control for the Web or desktop, in many cases it's easier to load your data into Microsoft Excel and use Power Maps to plot the data right on flat and globe maps of the earth. In Chapter 10, we show you what's possible with Power Maps and Excel.

What You Need to Get Started

We assume you're relatively proficient with writing applications for Microsoft platforms. Ideally, you're a developer proficient with Microsoft technologies, and you've had some experience with C# and the .NET platform—either native or server-side apps—and are comfortable using Microsoft Visual Studio. We're focused on making you proficient with the various location, mapping, and spatial facilities Microsoft makes available, rather than focusing on nuances of C# or building a native or Web-based application. At the same time, if we're doing anything particularly clever with a language feature or an interface, we'll be sure to explain what we're doing and why, so you can benefit from our experience. Similarly, when we discuss the Bing Maps for iOS control, we assume you have some rudimentary iOS experience.

Of course, you'll also need a way to develop for Microsoft platforms if you want to build on Microsoft's technologies in your application. At a minimum, you'll need a copy of Microsoft Visual Studio: Visual Studio Express 2012 for Web is a good place to start for the web, and either Visual Studio Express 2012 for Windows 8, Windows Desktop, or Windows Phone for the native application development we discuss later in this book.

We've written these chapters to be mostly independent of each other, stitched together by the common theme of this book and a collection of sample applications that demonstrate what we're helping you learn as you read this book. On a first reading, a good start would be to read the remainder of this chapter, and then skip directly to the chapter that interests you the most.

A Few Words on Terminology

Before we continue, it's worth getting a few bits of terminology straight, because depending on where you look, you're going to see some vocabulary that may be unfamiliar.

First, we generally use the words *location*, *geospatial*, *spatial*, and *mapping* interchangeably when discussing the notion of adding geospatial data to an application. In the software industry, these words have settled into particular use in particular domains: Microsoft SQL Server's additions in 2008 included support for *geospatial* entities, for example, and you're going to see the word *mapping* appear a lot in the documentation for Bing Maps, while *location* is a frequently occurring buzzword when it comes to how geospatial data is incorporated into social applications like Facebook, Twitter, and Foursquare.

Second, there are a few cartographic notions worth reviewing. Any position on the Earth can be represented as a pair of coordinates—a latitude, indicating how far north or south of the equator the point is, and a longitude, indicating how far east or west of the prime meridian (which falls through Greenwich, UK) the point is. By convention, northern latitudes are positive; southern latitudes are negative, while eastern longitudes are positive and western longitudes are negative. (Be careful! People in the western hemisphere new to geospatial software often assume that western longitude is positive. It isn't.)

The Earth is round, which poses some problems when we think about mapping the Earth. First, our coordinate system breaks down at the poles and the International Date Line—at the poles, the latitude is +90 or –90, while all longitudes coexist at the actual poles. Perhaps more perplexing in more circumstances is what happens to longitude at the International Date Line; it's discontinuous there. At one point immediately to the west of the date line you'll have a longitude approaching +180; cross the line in an easterly direction and the sign flips, with a longitude of –180. This is one reason for Microsoft SQL Server's geography type; it takes these funky discontinuities in stride.

Another reason for the type, and a pitfall you're probably already aware of, is that you can't present a flat map of the Earth on a plane without distortions. Various *projections* (consisting of formulas mapping a point on a sphere to a point on a plane) of the sphere onto the plane exist; Bing Maps, like most maps you're used to, uses the Mercator projection, which has two key advantages. It's conformal, meaning that the shape of relatively small objects is preserved; it's also cylindrical: at any point on the map, north and south are always up and down, and east and west are always left and right. However, the math of the projection gives some problems at the poles; Mercator maps don't map the pole regions very well, which is why when you look at countries further north and south of the equator, they look bigger in area than they actually are.

While the Earth is round, it's not perfectly round: it's a little squashed at the poles. To model the shape more exactly than using a sphere, geographers introduce the notion of the *datum*, a mathematical shape that more closely represents the Earth. To precisely position a point on the Earth, I should give you not just its latitude and longitude (and elevation, if the position is above or below the surface of the Earth), but a reference to the datum the coordinates are in as well. Fortunately, nearly all systems today, including those you'll use from Microsoft and the positions returned by GPS receivers and cell phones are in the World Geodetic System (WGS) 1984 datum, so you won't have to do any fancy math to move coordinates from one datum to another datum under normal circumstances.

▪ **Note** Another datum you might encounter in your work is North American Datum 27 (NAD27), which is still in use by some U.S governmental agencies like the Federal Communications Commission. If you're plotting data from another source, it's crucial you find out what datum the coordinates are in and interconvert if necessary.

We touched on geocoding and reverse geocoding in a previous section as a feature of Bing Maps; to *geocode* a street address is to get the latitude and longitude for the street address, while *to reverse geocode* a latitude and longitude is to get the closest street address to the point. By their very nature, these are approximate transformations, in practice you may find if you geocode an address and go to that point with a Global Positioning System (GPS) receiver that you're off by tens or hundreds of meters (even after taking into account the error in GPS), because addresses are often sequentially assigned to road segments assuming an equal spacing between addresses, rather than recognizing the nasty reality that parcel sizes may change, addresses may be skipped, and so on. If you're developing an application for another country, geocoding may be more or less accurate than it is in the United States, because of how addresses get assigned; some in-location testing is probably in order.

Speaking of different countries, it's worth noting that some jurisdictions have very specific laws or regulations about what kinds of geospatial information can be presented, recorded, or used. As of this writing, for example, there are restrictions in China both on where map data is stored (map providers like Microsoft must keep data about China in data centers inside China) and how the data can be presented on maps in software applications. If you're seeking to develop an application with international reach, or are specifically targeting one of those markets, you should stop and get the advice of a qualified legal professional early in your development cycle to make sure your business case meshes well with the legal climate.

Finally, this book is a book about writing software; the usual conventions apply for how you should read the print of the book, Words like this in a paragraph indicate a snippet of code such as a method or variable; when we present listings (which you don't need to type in, as the source code is available from the Apress web site) to illustrate points, we'll set them out like this:

Listing 1-1. Hello World, in C#.

```
public class Hello
{
    public static void Main()
    {
        System.Console.WriteLine("Hello, World!");
    }
}
```

Introducing the Sample Application

It doesn't take much these days to come up with an application idea that can be improved by the judicious use of location—we think that's why you bought this book! Throughout the book, we hang most of our examples on a suite of sample applications based on the same use case: tracking and reporting statistics about earthquakes. We show you how to do this using the SQL Database service on Azure, hosting the service on Azure, and presenting the data using the Web, Windows Presentation Foundation (WPF) for Windows 7.0, and as applications for Windows 8 using the Windows Store UI and Windows Phone, as well as showing the same data in Power Maps with Excel. In addition, we've created several smaller applications that show specific features of the Bing Maps API on specific clients, such as the reverse geocoding, routing, and traffic interfaces as well.

Before we dive into the next chapter and get you started with hosting your service on Azure, let's take a moment and look at the overall architecture for our main sample application; that way, as you read this book you understand the fundamental points and can focus on the Microsoft mapping details along the way. Figures 1-2(a) and 1-2(b) show the WPF version of our sample application, first in its default state when launched and then after zooming in on a particular earthquake.

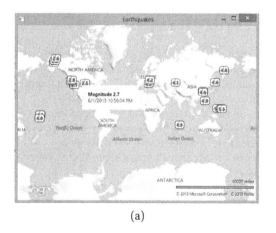
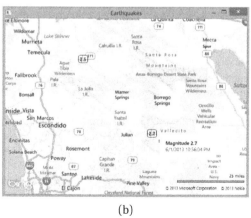

(a)	(b)

Figure 1-2. Our sample application, in (a) showing the entire world, in (b) after zooming in using the scrollwheel or pinch-to-zoom to see a particular area

The sample application is intentionally simple; its sole purpose is to provide a map populated with recent earthquakes around the world. You'll see this example again and again in this book, first as an application for the Web, and later as a native application for WPF, Windows Store (for Windows 8), and finally as a Windows Phone application. (You'll also see chunks of other sample applications, demonstrating other Bing Maps features such as traffic layers, routing, and geocoding.) When you launch the application, it immediately draws a map of the world and fetches recent earthquake data from our Azure service; you can zoom in on any area, pan the map, or hover over a marker to get more information about a specific earthquake record.

Figure 1-3 shows a block diagram of the overall architecture we've chosen for this sample application. It's admittedly more than the back end for our earthquake monitoring clients requires, but it lets us share with you important details about setting up services for location-based applications, hosting on Windows Azure, writing applications that communicate between client and server, and of course the client applications themselves.

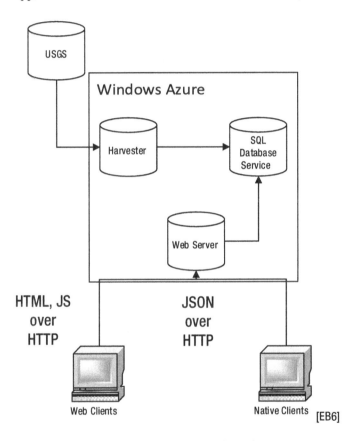

Figure 1-3. *The architecture for our sample application*

The components you see are:

- The USGS provides the raw earthquake data. Served as a comma-delimited file (CSV) over HTTP, each file contains a list of earthquakes and data about each earthquake over the last 24-hour period.

- The Harvester is a process running on Windows Azure that periodically polls the USGS for earthquake data and inserts records into the SQL database. (In a production application, it might also perform work such as purging the database of old records, or that might be left to other maintenance processes).

- The SQL database storing our earthquake data runs on the Azure SQL Database Service as a single database, with rows for each earthquake harvested by the harvester.

- The web server, running in Microsoft IIS, serves both the HTML and JavaScript for web clients using the service and provides a Windows Communication Foundation (WCF) service serving the same data to both web and native clients using JavaScript Object Notation (JSON) over the HyperText Transfer Protocol (HTTP).

- Application clients come in two flavors: web and native. The web client loads its application directly from the web server as JavaScript with HTML and image resources; the native clients run locally on a Windows 7, Windows 8, or Windows Phone host. All clients use the same WCF bindings, making integration dead-simple for the Windows applications, and only a little more difficult for the iOS platforms.

It's worth taking a few minutes to explain why we chose this architecture. First, there are more pieces than you'd need just to browse earthquake data from the USGS: you could just as easily pull the data directly from the USGS and display it on a map with Power Maps, which is what we do in Chapter 10. This is a reasonable approach, but not sufficient for our purposes, where we hope to show you how to build and deploy a Windows Azure service for your application.

In a real production service, your entire web service may live on Azure, or you may be dependent on legacy or enterprise services running in another data center. If that's the case, you need to bridge the gap somehow. We chose to bridge this gap using our harvester process, because one of our goals is to show you how to use the geospatial features in Microsoft's various database products. Our harvester polls the USGS and inserts earthquake records in our database; your bridge may do something similar, replicating an existing database. More likely—and more efficiently—your bridge running on Azure can make Web service calls to your legacy services, leaving the database on Azure for your client-specific operations not related to the legacy service. (In fact, your legacy server might also be a Microsoft SQL Server instance of some kind, and you might choose to host your geospatial data there.)

For large-scale services, you should consider replicating your SQL server on multiple hosts, either in your enterprise data center or in different zones of Microsoft Azure. We don't explicitly discuss replication in this book; for that, you should consult any of the good books on Microsoft SQL Server administration. However, it's important to recognize that the database can be a single point of failure for your entire service, so distributing this asset is a key component when building a large-scale service.

Equally important is distributing the front end to your service. As we discuss in the next chapter, when we explore Windows Azure in more detail, Azure has the notion of web hosts and worker hosts. Our harvester runs on a worker host, an instance of a machine responsible for doing batch computation, rather than serving client endpoints. In production environments, you'd replicate the web host providing the front end services multiple times, placing them behind one of Azure's load balancers configured to distribute client requests among multiple hosts. When you do this, you need to remember that client-server requests should be *stateless*, that is, they should be atomic and not rely on a persistent connection or sequence. This lets the load balancer make the most of your service, and ensures that if a web server goes down (or its connection is interrupted during the course of normal services) that the failover to another service can happen with a minimum of difficulty and no sign to the user that a transaction failed.

What kind of clients you choose for your application is largely a business decision. In our case, we wanted to show you the full range of platforms that Bing Maps supports, so we wrote clients for the web as well as the native clients that can host a Bing Maps control. Enterprise developers may choose to only support one or two platforms: say a native application using WPF or the Web, and a mobile application for mobile workers running on Windows Phone. If you're exclusively targeting Windows, you have an important decision to make: do you ship your application through the Windows Store and focus on Windows 8 users, or do you package your application and distribute it yourself, likely as a WPF application that runs on Windows 7 and Windows 8? Or do you do both, providing legacy Windows 7 users a means to access your service as well as supporting the more modern user interface paradigms in Windows 8? This decision is tricky, and likely will involve both programmers (who provide the cost estimates to build and maintain all of these applications) and business people (who should have an understanding of your target market and what platforms your prospective customers are actually using).

Developing Your Application

Developing a location-aware application is similar in process to developing any application. If your development team is small, or a one-man operation, be prepared to wear a lot of hats: database administrator, Web service developer, and client application developer. If you're building a larger application, or part of a team, a good way to divide and conquer the application development space is to partition it into three broad teams: *content*, *cloud*, and *client*:

- The content team is responsible for identifying and capturing any content your application needs. For example, if your application is a restaurant table reservation service, this team is responsible for identifying the restaurants you serve (likely a sales function) as well as developing the database schema and database for that content. Or maybe you're writing a location-aware game, and you need to capture locations that provide the setting and environment of the game; in that case, the content team is responsible for determining what data is germane to each setting, how it's stored, and so forth. You'll want content and database experts working together on this team.

- The cloud team builds the web services necessary to support the clients. It reaches into the content database over a well-defined interface to get what it needs on the one side, and serves that content to clients through a well-defined interface (likely WCF-hosted) on the other. Developers on this team should have good understanding of Azure and service deployment, and be able to write server-side applications fluently.

- The client team builds the clients that use the cloud team's web service. The responsibilities of this team vary depending on the kind of clients you need to support; maybe all you need is a crackerjack ASP.NET programmer and a good web page designer, or maybe you need native application development teams to target a number of platforms.

Dividing your work this way makes sense even if you're a small team; you can change roles depending on the phase of development you're in or what needs doing that day. It's easier to think about the complexities of a location-based application if you break down the pieces into manageable chunks, and these three chunks give you a good place to start. Of course, a larger effort may have multiple teams in each category; maybe you've got different client teams targeting the web, Apple iOS, and Windows Phone. Or maybe you're in the business of producing a lot of content (think of a service like Yelp) with sophisticated requirements for collecting and storing the content your service offers.

We're big fans of agile development, with one caveat: you need to take some care in defining the interfaces between each portion of your application, and spend some time up front making sure that you have a good database architecture in hand. In some software companies, agile is a substitute for no design; we prefer a model where small design tasks (say, identifying the interfaces the client will use to connect to the cloud) are estimated just the same as software tasks, and some lightweight documentation accompanies the final product. A model like scrum works particularly well for this, as you can iteratively refine each functional area if you're a small team in successive sprints, or run simultaneous scrum teams for each functional area at the same time, and then integrate the results with integration sprints between developing your core features.

Wrapping Up

While many firms provide the pieces you need to assemble a location-aware application for the web, desktop, or mobile client, only Microsoft offers an end-to-end solution that includes:

- A database (Microsoft SQL Server) with geospatial support for flat-map and round-earth coordinate systems, capable of storing and querying points and regions.

- A PaaS (Windows Azure) for hosting your database (using Azure's SQL Database Service) and cloud computing requirements, including state-of-the-art Web hosting with Microsoft IIS.

- Client-side map-rendering controls (Bing Maps) for the web, WPF, Windows Store, and Windows Phone applications.

- Web services to support your application including traffic, routing, geocoding, and reverse geocoding features.

The remainder of this book shows you how you can build your application with each of these pieces, giving you the skills you need to make your own location-aware applications. In the next chapter, we'll dig in to Windows Azure, so fasten your seat belt and prepare to take off into the cloud!

CHAPTER 2

Painless Hosting with Azure

In this chapter we show you how to host a simple application that displays a Bing Map on Windows Azure, Microsoft's cloud computing platform. Cloud computing provides agile IT for businesses and developers. If a business wanted to deploy a new web application, the traditional method of deployment would require that the business set up the necessary hardware, software, operations, and support team in order to host this application on premise. With cloud computing, all of the infrastructure needed to deploy that application would already be available on the cloud, thereby reducing the necessary setup time and money to deploy.

Why Windows Azure?

The main benefit of moving to the cloud is the savings in time and infrastructure for application deployment. You can focus on your application development and not the infrastructure. The backend is fully automated and handles the patching, updating, and maintenance of the operating system and applications. Windows Azure follows a pay-per-use model, where you only pay for the resources that your application uses; there is no upfront cost. One major concern in application deployment is the ability to survive hardware and system failures, and Windows Azure is designed with high availability in mind. Applications are replicated across multiple servers in different locations for fail-safe recovery. Microsoft delivers a 99.95% monthly SLA (Service-Level Agreement).

As is often the goal, your application may at times require scaling up as demands grow. Windows Azure is designed for elastic scale, therefore, multiple instances can be spun up as needed. Alternatively, the customer can drop the number of instances to zero when there is no demand. Since Windows Azure follows the pay-per-use model, you only pay for the number of instances that you use and the storage you consume. Another important benefit is that SQL Database (formerly SQL Azure), which is the storage component of Windows Azure, shares the same basic programming models with Microsoft SQL Server, thus if you are familiar with SQL Server product code base, your skills can be applied to working with SQL Database.

While a relatively new business for Microsoft, the growth of Windows Azure is a testament to the growing importance of cloud computing as well as Microsoft's platform. As of April 2013, Microsoft announced that Windows Azure had crossed the $1 billion threshold (see `http://bloom.bg/10JDhtG`), with over 200,000 customers.

Cloud Computing Services

Cloud computing refers to the notion of placing computing services in a central data center, accessible by the Internet. The main types of cloud computing services are Infrastructure as a Service (IaaS), Platform as a Service (PaaS), and Software as a Service (SaaS).

- IaaS provides the hardware necessary for deploying an application, however the onus is on the developer (customer) to patch, upgrade, and maintain the operating system.

- With PaaS, in addition to the hardware, the operating system and runtime environment necessary for deploying an application is also provided.

- Finally, SaaS provides the entire end-to-end software application to the customer. The customer is only required to sign up for a given service, and the SaaS handles the entire application for her.

We should note that there are in fact other types of cloud services such as Security as a Service or IT as a Service offered by other cloud computing platforms. The types of services available with Windows Azure are virtual machines (VMs) (IaaS), cloud application services (PaaS), and websites (SaaS) as in Figure 2-1.

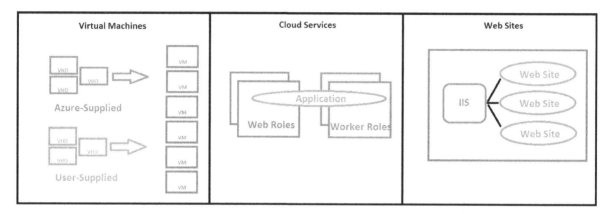

Figure 2-1. *Compute Services offered by Windows Azure*

Virtual Machines (IaaS)

Rather than requiring an actual on-premise physical machine, you can create VMs on demand—either from an image you supply or from a standard image. To create a VM, you simply specify which Virtual Hard Disk (VHD) to use and the size of the VM. Once you've done that, you define a VM role for your application. Essentially, Azure provides you with a server in the cloud that you can control and manage. You can deploy any available instance of Windows Server or Linux. Each VM will have your virtual hard desk (VHD) and it can contain your customized settings as well as your applications. You can make changes to these settings and applications while a VM is running, and the change is persisted such that the next time you create a VM from that VHD, the changes will be reflected. Alternatively, you can copy the changed VHD out of the cloud and run it locally.

There are different ways in which Windows Azure can be used. Firstly, you can use them to create inexpensive development and test platforms. Additionally, you can create and run applications that use any of the data management options provided by Windows Azure in conjunction with either SQL Server or another DBMS running in your VM. Finally, you can even use VMs as an extension of an on-premise datacenter. Windows Azure's VMs, in essence, provide the highest level of flexibility for those who would like to have access to many machines and full control of their management.

Cloud Services (PaaS)

A slightly less flexible service is a cloud service. In this case, you are given full control over your application; however you are exempt from the work required for administration. Applications can be deployed in Azure using languages such as C#, Java, PHP, Python, or Node.js in a VM running a version of Windows Server. To clarify, with the VMs described in the previous subsection, you must define the VM infrastructure, with cloud services, you are given a predefined VM on which you can deploy your applications. Azure will handle all of the management of this VM including restarting any VMs that fail.

There are two types of roles to choose from for cloud services: Web and Worker roles. A web role is for a front-end/web server. For example, you might have an ASP.NET enabled website. In this case, you use the Web role and upload the website code to the cloud. Azure will automatically deploy the website to the Azure Virtual Machine (VM) instances, and provide load balancing between the instances you've created.

Websites (SaaS)

Offering the last amount of flexibility are the SaaS Windows Azure Websites. This service allows you to build a scalable website using any operating system and ASP.Net, PHP, or Node.js and then deploy this website on the cloud. You manage the web environment using Microsoft Internet Information Service (IIS). You can either create a new website directly in the cloud, or you can move an existing IIS web site onto Windows Azure, as we will do in the example in this chapter. You can have multiple instances of the website running, and you can remove or add these instances even as the website is running. Additionally, Azure allows you to load balance the requests to the website across the various instances for higher performance.

As you have just read, Windows Azure provides you with the types of services that you can tailor to your needs. In fact, you can use one, two, or all three of these types of services in conjunction depending on your needs. Moreover, at all times Windows Azure has focused on providing a highly reliable cloud solution to you. As such, your VMs and applications are spread out across various locations and replicated for redundancy to safeguard against hardware failures and other such disasters.

At times you may want to have parts of your solution hosted on Azure but the remainder of it on premises. The **AppFabric** is the glue that connects these parts together by allowing you to integrate the Windows Azure applications with the on-premises application. You can leverage the **Service Bus** to enable communication between the cloud and on-premise applications. Alternatively, you can use the AppFabric's **Access Control Service** to create highly secure authorization for applications. Essentially, the AppFabric is a framework for managing and monitoring the applications running in the cloud.

Windows Azure Data Management

Azure also offers data services that allow you to store your data on the cloud. As you can see in Figure 2-2, the types of storage options are blobs, tables, and SQL databases. They are accessible via REST API calls or standard HTTP calls. Before we describe each of these types of storage, it is important to note that once again Windows Azure allows you to only pay for the amount of storage you use per month. Moreover, while the storage can be accessed by your Azure applications, it can also be accessed by applications running on your own local machines.

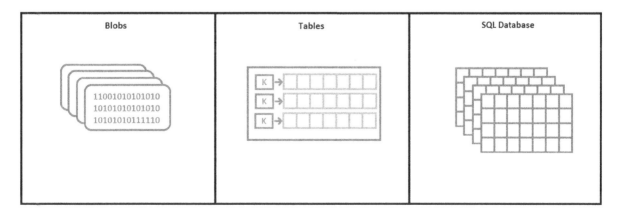

Figure 2-2. *Windows Azure offers different types of data storage: Blobs, tables, and SQL Databases*

Blobs

Blobs (**B**inary **L**arge **Ob**jects) are unstructured text or binary data such as images, audio, or videos. This type of storage is inexpensive, and a single blob can be as large as one terabyte. Blobs are grouped into containers and your account can have an unlimited number of containers, and each container can contain an unlimited number of blobs. The only restriction is that the total size of all blobs be less than 100TBs for a single storage account. In Figure 2-3, there are 9 blobs in that one account, of which there are 3 types of containers (image, audio, and video), and 5 distinct containers.

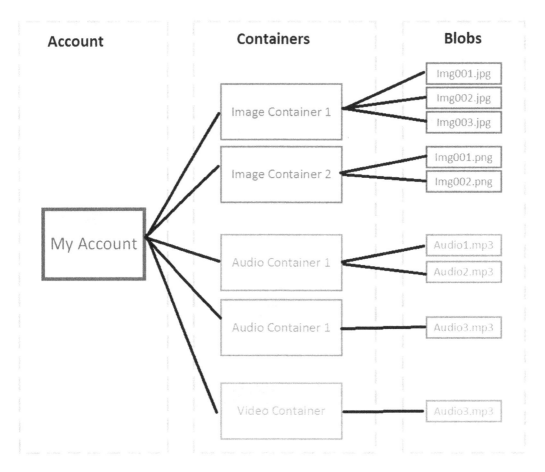

Figure 2-3. *Example of blob storage. Each account can have an unlimited number of containers, and containers can contain an unlimited number of blobs of the same type*

Tables

Tables are large amounts of structured but non-relational data, as shown in Figure 2-4. For example, you may wish to store a large amount of data that does not require you to perform SQL queries on this data, but you would still like fast access to it. In this case, tables are a good choice of data storage. Groups of data, such as dates, can be accessed by a unique key to that group. This type of storage is far less expensive than SQL Databases, but still provides you the ability to randomly access your data quickly.

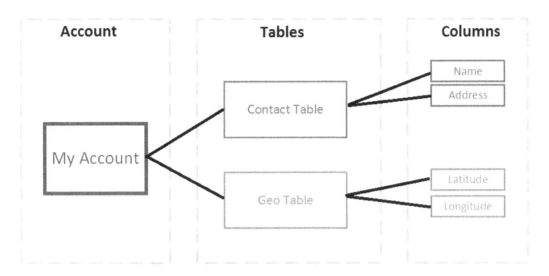

Figure 2-4. *Table storage in Azure is for non-relational data. An account can have from 0 to n tables associated with it*

SQL Databases

Finally, SQL databases are large amounts of structured and relational data. If you are familiar with using SQL Server then you are familiar with SQL Database. As with SQL Server, SQL Database can be accessed using a variety of data access tools such as ADO.NET or JDBC. SQL Database offers the added advantage of being a PaaS, in that while you can control the data and who can access it, Windows Azure takes care of managing all the hardware and infrastructure for you. Additionally, SQL Database federates the data across multiple servers, which is particularly useful for performance if your database receives large quantities of access requests.

In our example in this book, we will be storing blobs of geo data on the cloud. For the moment, in this chapter's example we will simply deploy an ASP.NET MVC on Azure.

Setting up Windows Azure

Getting started with Windows Azure is easy. You'll sign up for an account, download the Windows Azure SDK to your computer so you can use Microsoft Visual Studio to develop your Windows Azure applications, and that's it!

As you use the Windows Azure SDK, you can also model most of the Windows Azure features, including storage and hosting, right on your local development machine. This is especially handy when you're just starting development, because it lets you experiment with Windows Azure and your code without taking the time to spin up one or more virtual machines to host your services.

Getting a Windows Azure Account

Before you can begin developing your application, you will need a Windows Azure account. Microsoft has made this a painless, straightforward process. You can begin with signing up for a trial at `http://bit.ly/15tpYgF` (`http://www.windowsazure.com`), as shown in Figure 2-5, with a single click.

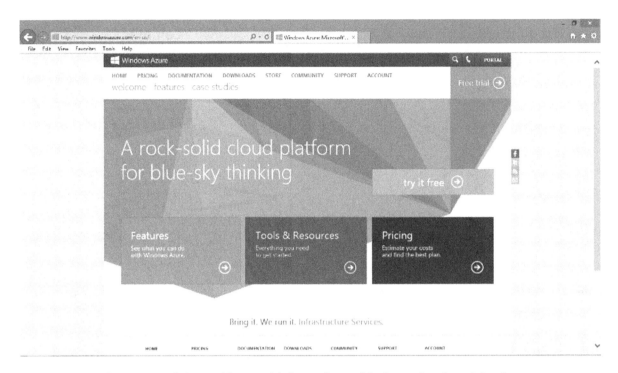

Figure 2-5. *Windows Azure website provides a straightforward way of signing up for a free trial and account*

■ **Note**   Microsoft experiments with different trial offers; when we wrote this, the trial was a three-month free trial—a great deal! Your mileage may vary, however, and if you're a member of MSDN, there may be a MSDN trial available as well.

You will be required to sign in with a **Windows Live ID**, which you can also sign up for if you do not yet have one. Once you have signed in, you will be redirected to the 90-day free trial page, as shown in Figure 2-6. You will need both a mobile phone as well as a credit card for signing up. You will not be charged on your credit card during the trial, it's just for verification and as a means for Microsoft to avoid spam botting. You will begin by entering a mobile phone number, to which a verification code will be sent. Once you verify your account with the code, you will be redirected to the credit card sign in page. After entering your credit card information, your sign in is complete.

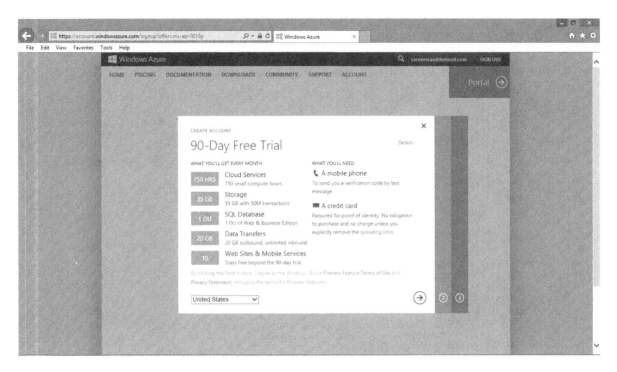

Figure 2-6. *Windows Azure 90-Day Free Trial sign up page*

Getting the Windows Azure SDK

Now that you've obtained a Windows Azure Account, you will want to install the Windows Azure SDK on your development machine. In this book, we will be using Visual Studio 2012, ASP.NET, and C#. Of course, ASP.NET is not the only web hosting language you can use with Windows Azure; Figure 2-7 shows the different SDKs you can install on your machine for development. Click on .NET, to install the SDK. If your machine already has Visual Studio 2010 installed, that is also acceptable, but be sure to install the corresponding SDK when given the option. Alternatively, if your machine does not have Visual Studio installed, the one-click installation will also install the Web Express edition on your machine.

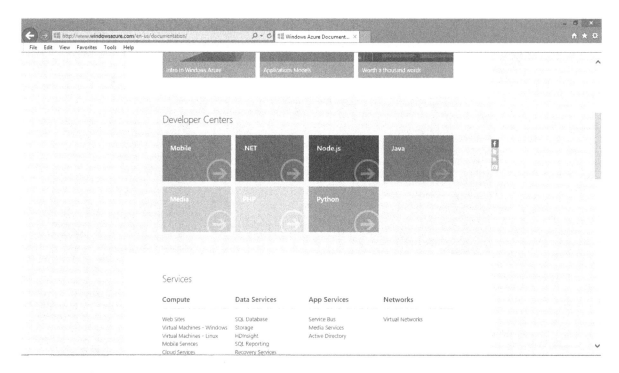

Figure 2-7. *The Windows Azure website provides easy one-click installation for various SDKs for Windows Azure development*

Hosting a Bing Map on Azure

To make sure you've set everything up correctly, let's create a simple web page that just shows a map using the Bing Maps AJAX control.

Obtaining a Bing Maps Account

In order to work with Bing Maps, you will need to obtain Bing Maps account, if you do not already have one. You can do so at `http://bit.ly/ZmFU3q` (`https://www.bingmapsportal.com`). You will need to click on **create** in the New User box. Once again you will need to sign in with your Windows Live ID account. Once you do so, you will need to provide an account name, a contact name, a company name, an e-mail address, a phone number, and agree to the Bing Maps terms of use. Once you have saved this information, you now have a Bing Maps Account.

Obtaining a Bing Maps Key

Even though you have an account, you still require a key in order to use the Bing Maps API. You can do so at the same site from which you obtained the Bing Maps account. If you are not already signed in, you will be prompted to sign in with your Windows Live ID. Once you do so, you can obtain a key by clicking on **Create or View Keys** under **My Account**. You will be required to fill out the form in Figure 2-8. The application name is required, as well as the type of key. In this book, we use a Basic key which is used for non-trial applications that do not exceed 50,000 transactions of any type within a 24-hour period. A Basic Key must comply with the Bings Maps Terms of Use, which you can read at `http://bit.ly/16Bx1bS`.

Figure 2-8. *Obtain a key to work with Bing Maps API by creating a key at* www.bingmapsportal.com

Once you submit the Create key form, you will then have a key you can use with the Bing Maps API. It should resemble this string:

```
XX_XXXxX_x_XXXXXXXX-XXXXXXXXX-1xXxXxXXXXXxXXxx-xxXxXXXXxxx_xXXX
```

■ **Note**   Make sure you stick a copy of your Bing Maps Key someplace handy, as you'll need it a lot when working through the sample code in this book.

With this string you are now ready to use the Bing Maps API to build our sample application.

Building the Bing Map

Now that you have a Bing Map API key, you are ready to begin using the Bing Map API to build your map. Microsoft offers a Bing Map API interactive SDK at the Bing Maps portal, `http://bit.ly/18HDak6`. From this portal, you can choose the types of features you would like to add to your map and get the corresponding HTML code listing to create such a map by clicking on **View HTML**, as seen in Figure 2-9.

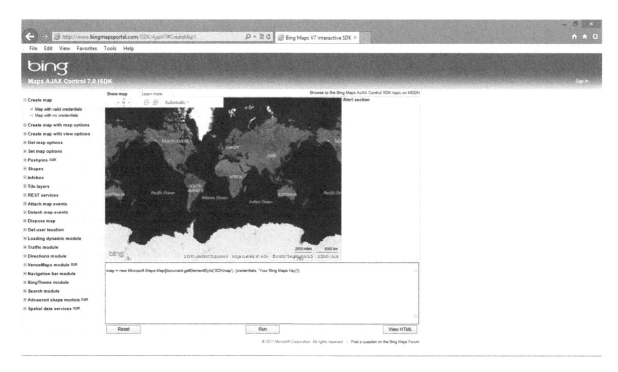

Figure 2-9. *Bing Map API Interactive SDK provides support for map creation*

For our example, we use the basic map with the correct credentials. The credential is the Bing Map key we obtained in the previous section. You will replace the string "Your Bing Maps Key" with the key. Thus, your HTML listing will look like the code in Listing 2-1. You will then be able to save this listing as an HTML file and view it in a browser. We have saved this listing as **Map.htm**. This map has basic zoom functionality as well as the option to switch between road and aerial (Bird's Eye) view.

Listing 2-1. Map.htm, HTML code for a basic Bing Map with valid credentials

```
<!DOCTYPE html PUBLIC "-//W3C//DTD XHTML 1.0 Transitional//EN"
"http://www.w3.org/TR/xhtml1/DTD/xhtml1-transitional.dtd">
<html>
   <head>
      <title>Map with valid credentials</title>
      <meta http-equiv="Content-Type" content="text/html; charset=utf-8"/>
      <script
         type="text/javascript"
         src="http://ecn.dev.virtualearth.net/mapcontrol/mapcontrol.ashx?v=7.0">
      </script>
      <script type="text/javascript">
      var map = null;
```

```
function getMap()
{
    map = new Microsoft.Maps.Map(document.getElementById('myMap'),
    {
        credentials:
        'XX_XXXxX_x_XXXXXXXX-XXXXXXXX-1xXxXxXXXXXXxXXxx-xxXxXXXXxxx_xXXX'
    });
}
</script>
</head>
<body onload="getMap();">
    <div id='myMap' style="position:relative; width:400px; height:400px;"></div>
</body>
</html>
```

Hosting the Bing Map on Windows Azure

Now that you have created the map, we will show you how to programatically host it on Windows Azure.

In Visual Studio, create a new ASP.NET MVC 4 Web Application project for C#, as in Figure 2-10. We save the project as **BingMapOnAzure**.

Figure 2-10. *Visual Studio 2012, create a ASP .NET MVC 4 Web Application*

Select the **Internet Application** template. This template generates the code for creating a basic MVC web application, with a web page that looks like Figure 2-11.

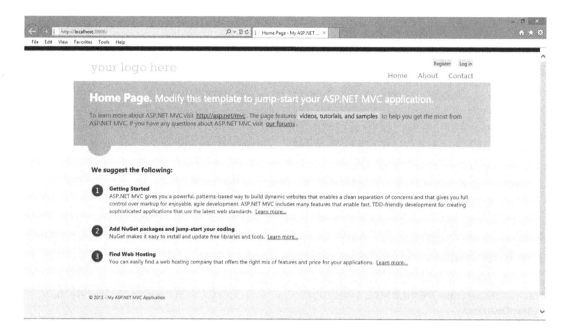

Figure 2-11. *Basic MVC Web Application web page generated by the code template from Visual Studio*

We will now modify this template code to host the Bing map you generated in the previous section. In the current template, there are different tabbed pages: **Home**, **About,** and **Contact**. We will modify the map over the **About** page. First, in the listing you will change the name of the page from **About** to **Map** in both the code listing and the **About**. **cshtml** file name to **Map.cshtml** in the Solution Explorer, as in Figure 2-12.

Figure 2-12. *Change the webpage name and file name from About to Map*

In **_Layout.cshtml**, change the action link parameters from About to Map, see Figure 2-13.

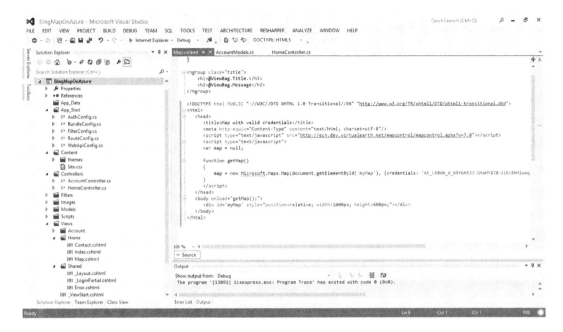

Figure 2-13. *Change the link About to Map*

In Map.cshtml, paste the Bing map code listing from Listing 2-1, as shown in Figure 2-14.

Figure 2-14. *Map.cshtml with Bing map code listing from Listing 2-1*

Now we will convert the code template to be Azure enabled to be able to deploy the project on Windows Azure. In order to do that, you right-click on the project in the Solution Explorer and select **Add Windows Azure Cloud Service Project,** as shown in Figure 2-15. By doing so, we have now added into the solution another project that by default is called **BingMapOnAzure.Azure**. This project will manage the deployment settings and configuration settings required to deploy on Azure. You can now run this project on Azure, or the Azure emulator that came with the Azure SDK you have installed on your machine.

Figure 2-15. *To Azure enable the project, right-click on Add Windows Azure Cloud Service Project*

Once the project is Azure enabled, to deploy on Azure, right-click on the project and select **Publish**. You will be brought to the Publish Sign In page, Figure 2-16. You must add your Azure account credentials here. To do so, you must be signed in to your Windows Live ID. If you are not already signed in, you will be brought to the sign-in page in your web browser. Once you sign in, it will automatically download your credentials to your machine. Save the file somewhere you can find it again. Import this file in the Publish Sign In page.

Figure 2-16. *Windows Azure Publish Sign In page. Click Import to add your credentials*

The next step is to create your cloud service. In the Publish Sign In page and Settings, as in Figure 2-17, we named our cloud service BingMapOnAzure, and chose the location of West US. Click **OK** and then **Publish** and deployment to Azure will begin.

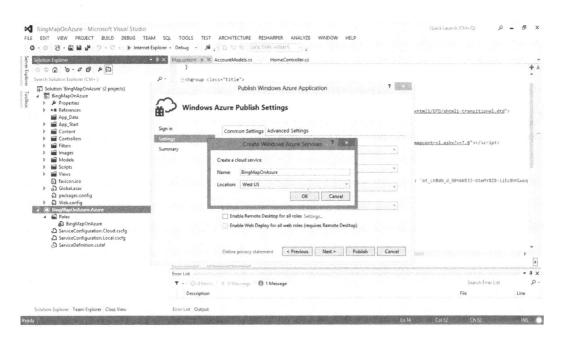

Figure 2-17. *Create a cloud service*

■ **Note**   The exclamation point   in the Windows Azure Activity Log beside the deployment status is not a warning or caution sign, do not be alarmed by it. It is an unfortunate choice of icon to indicate that the deployment is ongoing.

Once the deployment is complete, you can click on the link for the website in Windows Azure Activity Log: `http://bingmaponazure.cloudapp.net`, as in Figure 2-18.

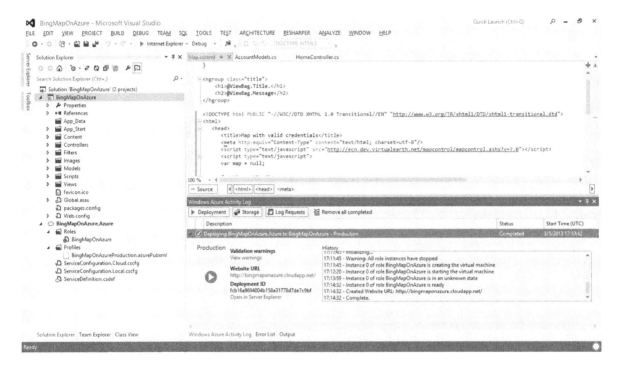

Figure 2-18.   *Once the deployment is complete, you can click on the Website URL*

By clicking on the Website URL, the resulting application that is running on Azure will open in the web browser. Figure 2-19 shows the Bing Map application running in a web browser.

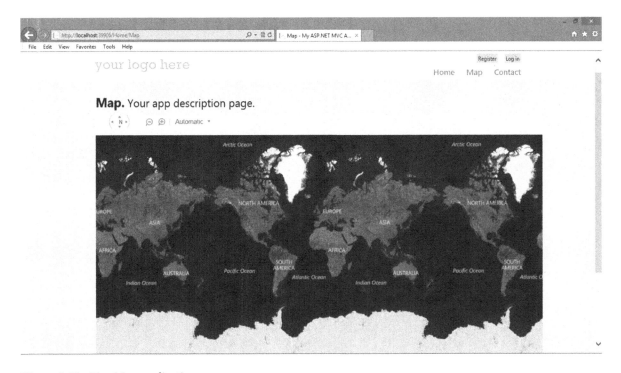

Figure 2-19. *Bing Map application*

Wrapping Up

In this chapter we learned about hosting on Windows Azure. Windows Azure is a robust, easy to install, cost-effective solution for those looking to manage their own virtual machines in the cloud, deploy applications while leaving the management of the operating system to Azure, or simply host websites in the cloud. Using a cloud-based solution, you can avoid all the costs associated with hosting things on-premises such as hardware, infrastructure, and support team. Additionally, Azure follows a pay-per-usage model, where you only pay for what you use, thereby significantly reducing cost. Azure also was built with reliability and robustness in mind. Your data, and applications are replicated over several servers in various different physical locations, to protect you from any hardware failures or other disasters that could occur. The other advantage of Azure is the ease of use. Installation is done on a single click! Any developer who is familiar with .NET is already primed for programming to deploy in Azure. Alternatively, you can also develop in Node.js or even PHP.

The example in this chapter showed you how to install Windows Azure, obtain a Bing Maps Key, build a Bing Map in .NET, and finally deploy this map on Azure. In the following chapter we will show you how to get your geospatial data onto the Azure storage, and how to manage this data.

■ ■ ■

CHAPTER 3

Geospatial with Azure SQL Database

In this chapter, we will give you a brief overview of Azure's SQL Database and how it can be used to host your geospatial data. We will then present a sample application that takes the geospatial earthquake data from http://earthquake.usgs.gov/earthquakes/ and stores it on the SQL Database.

SQL Database Overview

If you are familiar with SQL Server then transitioning to Azure SQL Database is straightforward as the latter is just the cloud-based implementation of a relational database that is built on top of Microsoft SQL Server. You will often find that SQL Database is referred to as SQL Azure in many books and online resources. For all intents and purposes, they are one and the same, and you can think of SQL Azure as the former name of SQL Database, and SQL Database as the updated version of SQL Azure.

There are a few key differences between SQL Server and SQL Database. With SQL Server, it is hosted on premise and you are responsible for the administration of both the database as well as the physical hardware. SQL Database abstracts the logical from the physical administration, so you are only responsible for the administration of the databases, logins, users, and roles. Hardware such as the hard drives, servers, and storage are all taken care of by Windows Azure. In addition to removing the responsibility of obtaining and maintaining hardware, the benefit of using SQL Database over SQL Server is that you have access to a service that is highly scalable, highly available, highly secure, and highly reliable. Scalability is made possible because SQL Database enables you to spin up as many virtual machines as you require. Availability is made possible because SQL Database handles the load balancing for you. And security and reliability are possible because SQL Database replicates your data across different locations and Windows Azure automatically handles the security for you.

Your databases may reside on different physical computers at the Microsoft data center. One key difference is that because your data is automatically replicated, and you do not have access to the computer's file systems; the SQL Server backup and restore commands are not applicable to SQL Database. You are, however, permitted to copy your entire database to a new database in SQL Database. With on-premise SQL Server setups, you are responsible for preparing the server with the appropriate systems, data, and software to make it ready for network operation. SQL Database handles this provisioning process for you. And you can begin this process immediately after you create your Windows Azure account.

Accessing Data in SQL Database

There are two ways of accessing data in the SQL Database, as seen in Figure 3-1:

- Application is hosted on premise and uses Tabular Data Streams (TDS) over a secure sockets layer (SSL) to transfer data from the SQL Database

- Application is hosted on Windows Azure and the database also resides on Windows Azure
  This is the scenario we are using in this chapter. You will use a web-based client and the WCF Data Services to access the application and data hosted on Azure.

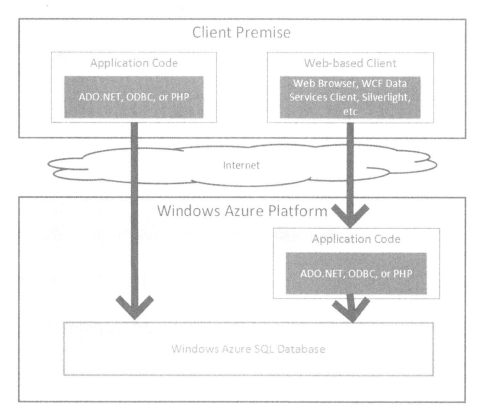

Figure 3-1. *Two options for accessing data in the SQL Database: application code is on premise, and application code is in the cloud*

Both options are viable options but come with different implications. When you host your application on-premise, one major issue is network latency. Traditionally, both your application and your server would be hosted on-premise; however, if you move your server to the cloud, then you must consider the latency of trafficking the data between the server and the application. By hosting both your application and your database in Azure, you minimize the network latency of requests to the database.

SQL Database Architecture.Overview

The SQL Database architecture is divided into four layers: the client layer, the service layer, the platform layer, and the infrastructure layer. Figure 3-2 shows these layers.

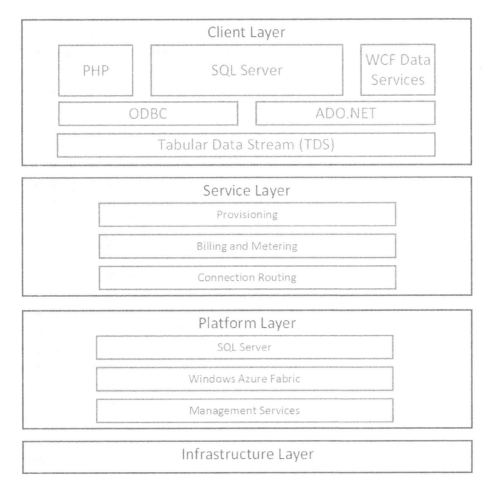

Figure 3-2. *SQL Database Architecture consists of four layers: Client, Service, Platform and Infrastructure Layer*

The Client Layer

The client layer can reside either on premise or on Azure. This is the layer that is closest to your application. SQL Database provides the same tabular data stream (TDS) interface as SQL servers; thus, the tools and libraries are familiar, if you are familiar with SQL server.

The Service Layer

The service layer provides three functions: provisioning, billing and metering, and connection routing.

- **Provisioning:** Provisions the databases with the necessary systems, data and software so that the database is ready for network use.

- **Billing and metering:** The billing and metering is what monitors each Windows Azure account's usage. This service is what allows multi-tenant support on SQL Database.

- **Connection routing:** Your data may reside on numerous physical servers. The service layer is what handles all the connections between your application and your data on the various servers.

The Platform Layer

The platform layer is where your data resides. It consists of many SQL server instances, each of which is managed by the SQL Database fabric. The SQL Database fabric is a distributed computing system made up of tightly integrated networks, servers, and storage. It handles the load balancing, automatic failover, and automatic replication of data between servers.

The Infrastructure Level

The infrastructure level handles the IT administration of the physical hardware and operating systems that support the services layer.

SQL Database Provisioning Model

As seen in Figure 3-3, a Windows Azure Platform can be associated with multiple SQL Database Servers and a SQL Database Server can be associated with multiple databases.

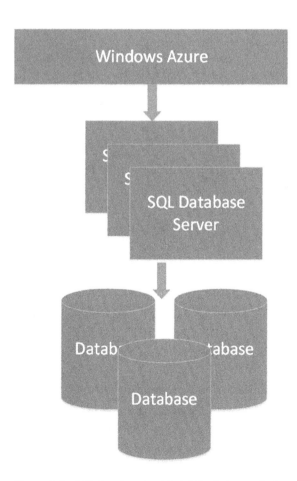

Figure 3-3. *SQL Provisioning Model: Each Azure platform is associated with multiple Servers, and each server can be associated with multiple databases*

A SQL Database server is a logical group of databases and handles the administration between multiple databases. The SQL Database server includes logins similar to those in instances of SQL Server. During the provisioning process, each SQL Database server is assigned a unique domain name, such as *servername.database.windows.net*, where *servername* is the name of the SQL Database server.

The databases are what contain the data using tables, views, indices, and other stored procedures. During the provisioning process, a master database is created, and it keeps track of which logins have permission to create databases or other logins. You must be connected to **master** in order to CREATE, ALTER, or DROP logins.

Federations in SQL Database

A federation is a collection of database partitions that are defined by a federation scheme that in turn defines a federation distribution key, which determines the distribution of data across the federated database partitions. Essentially it is a horizontal partition of your database. For example, in a 100-row database, rows 1 through 50 can be in one partition and rows 51 to 100 can be in another partition. A federation is used to achieve greater scalability and performance from the database portion of your application.

Each database partition within a federation is known as a federation member and has its own schema, and contains the federated table rows that correspond to its range. For example, in our earlier example, the federated table will contain rows 1 to 50 for the federated member containing the range 1 to 50. Federated tables are tables that are spread across federation members. Each member can also contain reference tables, which are not federation aware. In other words, the reference table is wholly contained within a member and usually contains information that is referenced in relation to the federated table within that member.

Federations are accessed through a federation root database. The root performs the routing to the appropriate federation members based on the given federation key value. Each root may contain multiple federations, each with its own federation scheme. The root database in Figure 3-4 points to two federations, each with two federated databases.

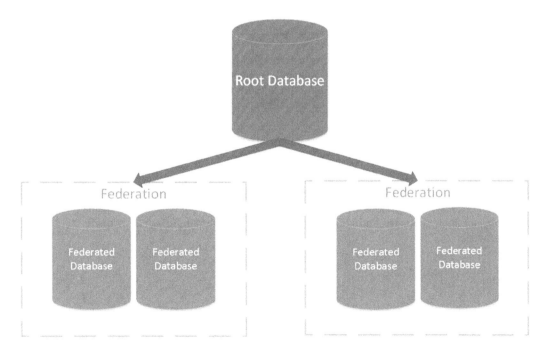

Figure 3-4. *A federation root database points to multiple federations. Each federation contains the federated databases*

Geospatial representation in SQL Database

Microsoft has had support for geospatial types since SQL Server 2008. By extension, SQL Database can represent and store geospatial data. Before we describe how geospatial data is represented in SQL Database, we will give you an overview of spatial reference systems.

Spatial Reference Systems Overview

A spatial reference system (SRS) is a system to represent a point on the earth uniquely. There are, in fact, many spatial reference systems, so it follows that there are many ways a point on the earth may be represented. An SRS must be able to specify types of coordinates used (such as latitude/longitude or easting/northing coordinates, specify from where those coordinates are measured, the units of the coordinates, and the shape of the earth over which those coordinates extend.

The earth is not a simple sphere, but a complex shape. Its shape is called a geoid and represents the earth and only the earth. Because it is such a complicated shape to represent, it is approximated using different ellipsoids. Each approximation affects the accuracy at different positions on the earth. Once the correct model ellipsoid is chosen, it must also be aligned with the earth by using a frame of reference. There are again, various frames of references defined. Together, the reference ellipsoid and the reference frame form a *geodetic datum*, of which the most known one is the *World Geodetic System of 1984 (WGS84)*.

Latitudes and longitudes are two of the more common ways of representing a point in space, it can be represented as a decimal (37.775192,−122.419381) or in degrees, minutes, and seconds (37° 46' 30.6906", -122° 25' 9.768"). The next challenge is to represent a 3D world on a 2D plane. That is where projection becomes important. Once again, there are different methods of projecting the earth onto a 2D plane of which the most common is the *Mercator Projection*. Both Bing and Google Maps use the Mercator projection.

SQL Database Spatial Data Types

Now that you have a slightly better idea of spatial references, we can show you how SQL Database supports this data. There are two types of spatial data supported by SQL Database: geometry and geography. The geometry data type supports planar or (flat-earth) data. The geography data type supports ellipsoidal (round-earth) data. Both the geometry and geography data types support various spatial data objects as depicted in Figure 3-5. The data objects can be categorized as follows:

- **Single geometries:** contain only one discrete geometric element. The single geometries represented by SQL Database are points (*Point*), curves (*LineString, CircularString, and Compound String*), and surfaces (*Polygon* and *CurvePolygon*).

- **Geometry collections:** contain one or more of the single geometries. There are two types of geometry collections: homogeneous and heterogeneous. A homogeneous collection contains only one type of single geometry, and a heterogeneous collection contains one or more of the single geometries.

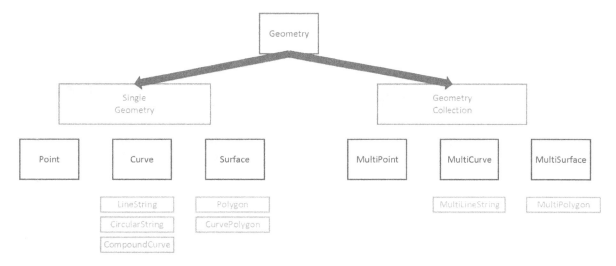

Figure 3-5. *SQL Database geometries are the same as SQL Server geometries*

Figure 3-5 depicts the different types of geometries that are supported by SQL Database.

While both geometry and geography data types support the same geometries, they differ in the way they represent the types. For example, both geometry and geography data types can represent an edge between two vertices, however, in the geometry type, the edge is a straight line, and in the geography type the edge is an elliptic arc.

SQL Database also provides methods for manipulating the spatial data types. There are methods for constructing geometry from Well-Known Text (WKT) Input:

- **STGeomFromText:** constructs any type of geometry instance from WKT input

- **STPointFromText:** constructs a geometry Point from WKT

- **STMPointFromText:** constructs a geometry MultiPoint from WKT

- **STLineFromText:** constructs a geometry LineString from WKT

- **STMLineFromText:** constructs a geometry MultiLineString from WKT

- **STPolyFromText:** constructs a geometry Polygon from WKT

- **STMPolyFromText:** constructs a geometry MultiPolygon from WKT

- **STGeomColFromText:** constructs a geometry GeometryCollection from WKT

There are also methods for constructing geometry from Well-Known Binary (WKB) Input,: which are the same functionality as the above methods other than the input: **STGeomFromWKB**, **STPointFromWKB**, **STMPointFromWKB**, **STLineFromWKB**, **STMLineFromWKB**, **STPolyFromWKB**, **STMPolyFromWKB**, and **STGeomColFromWKB**.

An example of how to call one of the above static methods is:

```
DECLARE @g geometry;
SET @g = geometry::STPointFromText('POINT (100 100)', 0);
SELECT @g.ToString();
```

In the sample application below, we will be using this very spatial type in order to represent a latitude and longitude.

Setting up a SQL Database

In this section we will describe how to setup a SQL Database. Much of the database can be setup and managed through the management portal. Alternatively, many tasks can be handled programmatically. For example, you may choose to create tables through the management portal associated with your Azure account, or you may create tables in your code. We will show you how to do both in this chapter. Complete the following steps to create a SQL Database:

1. Log on to your management portal on the www.windowsazure.com. As always, you will need your Windows Live ID to login. Your management portal should appear as in Figure 3-6. If you followed the example in Chapter 2, then you should have one service listed under **all items**. In our case, it is the bingmapsonazure webpage we created in Chapter 2.

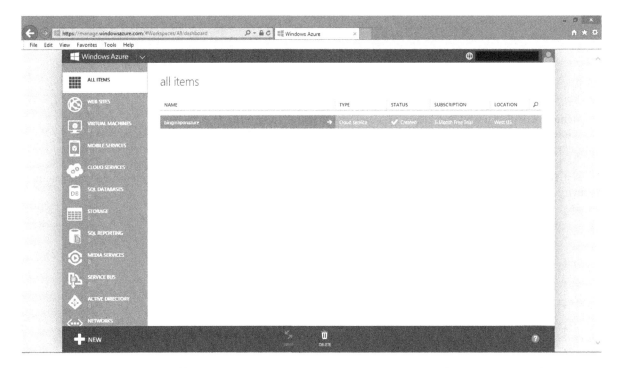

Figure 3-6. *Management portal for Windows Azure. In addition to handling your cloud services, you can also manage your storage here*

2. Click on SQL Databases on the left menu. If this is your first time, then you should have no SQL Databases in the portal, as is the case in Figure 3-7. You can click **CREATE A SQL DATABASE**, to create your first database.

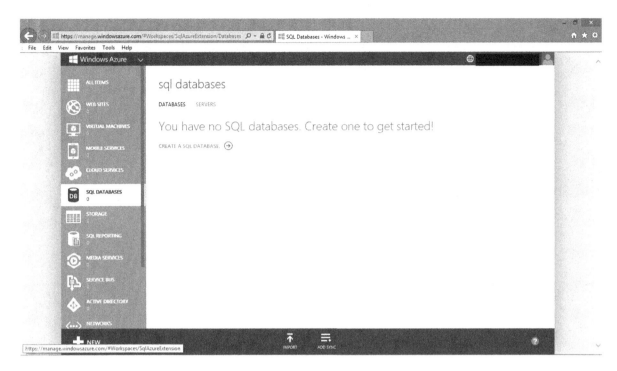

Figure 3-7. *There are no SQL Databases associated with this account. To create one, you click on* ***CREATE A SQL DATABASE***

3. You should name the database and choose a server. In Figure 3-8, we have named the database **EarthquakeMap** and selected a **New SQL database server**. As explained earlier, once you complete the creation process, Azure will provide a servername for you in the provisioning process.

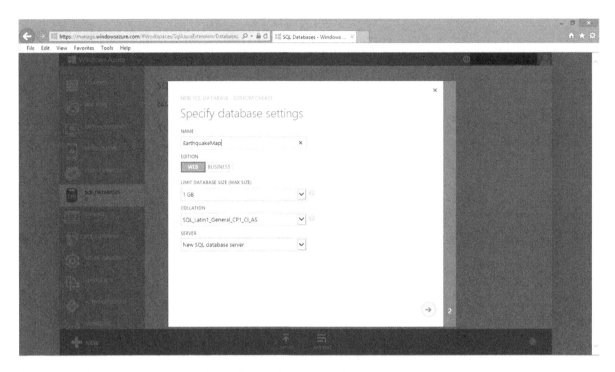

Figure 3-8. *You can select a name and type of server for your new database*

4. You will be asked to select a login name and password. Jot down what you've chosen, as you will be required to have the login information for interacting with the database.

5. Once you are done entering the server settings (login and password), you click on the check mark if you are satisfied with your choices, and you will have created your database! Your management portal will now list this database and server, as in Figure 3-9.

Figure 3-9. *The management portal lists the databases and servers associated with your account*

6. You now have to configure the firewall settings. You must add your IP to the list of allowable addresses by clicking **Add to the Allowed IP Addresses** and then clicking **save** at the bottom of the page, as seen in Figure 3-10.

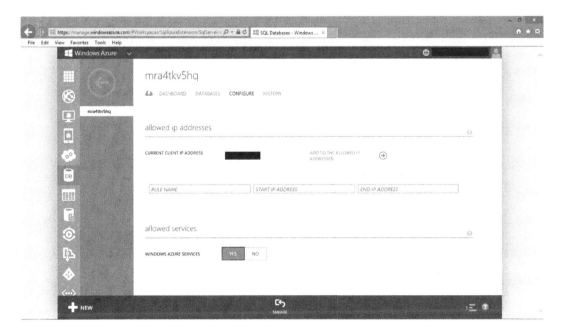

Figure 3-10. *Configure your firewall settings by adding your IP to the list of allowable addresses*

7. Go back to the SQL Database page by clicking the DB icon: [DB] .

8. Click on the white arrow listed by your database name to return to the management portal for the database.

sql databases

DATABASES   SERVERS

NAME	STATUS	LOCATION
EarthquakeMap →	✔ Online	West US

Figure 3-11. The created database as listed by the SQL Database management portal

9. The management portal for that database will appear as in Figure 3-12. From this portal, you can design your database, connect to your database, and run queries on this database, among other services.

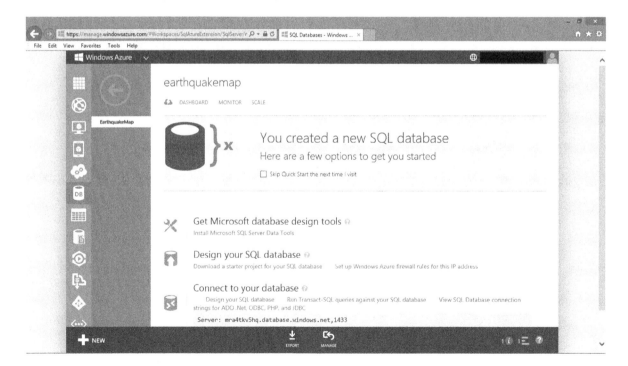

Figure 3-12. The management portal for the newly created database

10. Select the **MANAGE** icon at the bottom of the page. You will be prompted for your login and password created in step 4.

11. Start a new query by clicking on the **New Query** icon near the top of the page:

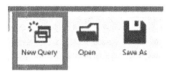

Figure 3-13. *Selecting New Query will allow you to query the newly created database*

If you do not see this option, you may have to select **Run Transact-SQL queries against your SQL database** from Figure 3-11.

12. You enter the query and hit run. In the following code listing we show you an example of how you can create a new table for the newly created database:

```
-- Create the earthquakeData table.
   IF NOT EXISTS (SELECT * FROM sys.objects
       WHERE object_id = OBJECT_ID(N'[dbo].[EarthquakeData]')
       AND type in (N'U'))
   BEGIN
   CREATE TABLE [dbo].[EarthquakeData](
       [DateTime] [datetime] NOT NULL,
       [Position] [Geography] NOT NULL,
       [Depth] [float] NOT NULL,
       [Magnitude] [float] NOT NULL,
       [MagType] [nvarchar](50) NOT NULL,
       [NbStation] [int] NOT NULL,
       [Gap] [int] NOT NULL,
       [Distance] [float] NOT NULL,
       [RMS] [float] NOT NULL,
       [EventID] [nvarchar](50) NOT NULL,
       [Source] [float] NOT NULL,
       [Version] [float] NOT NULL
       )
   END;
   GO
```

13. Click on Run to run the query and you now have a server that has one database that has one table!!

Inserting geospatial data into a SQL Database

In this section, we will be showing you how to insert data into your SQL Database. In our book example, we are creating an application that displays earthquake data. You can retrieve the daily updates of all the earthquakes that occurred in the previous 2.5 days at the following website: http://on.doi.gov/1cXCj1C. In Figure 3-14, you can see a sample CVS file containing the earthquake data.

	A	B	C	D	E	F	G	H	I	J	K	L	M
1	DateTime	Latitude	Longitude	Depth	Magnitude	MagType	NbStations	Gap	Distance	RMS	Source	EventID	Version
2	2013-06-21T02:21:18.310+00:00	51.183	156.564	139.9	4.6	mb	55	162	2.1	0.82	us	usc000hwy0	1.37178E+12
3	2013-06-21T00:07:09.000+00:00	62.221	-151.233	106.2	3.2	Ml				0.81	ak	ak10742812	1.37177E+12
4	2013-06-21T00:06:19.530+00:00	-26.933	-63.271	581.4	4.5	mb	41	90	5.4	0.81	us	usc000hww9	1.37177E+12
5	2013-06-20T23:56:48.000+00:00	40.175	-121.111	2.1	2.6	Md		79	0.3	0.36	nc	nc72012380	1.37179E+12
6	2013-06-20T23:06:06.000+00:00	62.236	-145.715	22.3	4.4	Ml				0.96	ak	ak10742749	1.37178E+12
7	2013-06-20T21:26:02.300+00:00	18.455	-67.223	96	2.6	Md	13	274	0.1	0.25	pr	pr13171006	1.37177E+12
8	2013-06-20T21:21:12.090+00:00	54.808	164.047	25.5	4.5	mb	24	154	3.7	0.7	us	usc000hwr4	1.37177E+12
9	2013-06-20T21:01:19.620+00:00	43.016	-110.819	5	3.1	ML	36	77	0.3	0.6	us	usc000hwpa	1.37178E+12
10	2013-06-20T17:38:36.000+00:00	19.339	-155.271	32.4	3	Ml		76	0	0.11	hv	hv60514101	1.37176E+12
11	2013-06-20T16:33:52.900+00:00	18.967	-65.14	17	3.2	Md	19	266	0.6	0.25	pr	pr13171003	1.37175E+12
12	2013-06-20T16:16:14.040+00:00	15.691	-87.154	25.1	4.3	mb	45	124	1.6	1.36	us	usc000hw3i	1.37177E+12
13	2013-06-20T16:04:19.000+00:00	51.733	179.214	103.9	2.5	Ml				0.39	ak	ak10742631	1.37176E+12
14	2013-06-20T15:06:21.645+00:00	39.111	-119.718	9.2	2.8	ml	34	80	0	0.12	nn	nn00415768	1.37178E+12
15	2013-06-20T14:19:28.000+00:00	18.745	-65.59	41	2.8	Md	13	227	0.5	0.17	pr	pr13171002	1.37174E+12
16	2013-06-20T13:39:24.000+00:00	51.768	-172.528	26.3	2.9	Ml				0.35	ak	ak10742601	1.37176E+12
17	2013-06-20T12:15:45.330+00:00	-21.21	-68.442	136.3	4.4	mb	12	107	1	0.68	us	usc000hvx1	1.37176E+12
18	2013-06-20T11:09:01.000+00:00	61.412	-149.973	33.5	3.1	Ml				1.15	ak	ak10742561	1.37176E+12
19	2013-06-20T09:05:14.470+00:00	49.773	125.246	14.8	4.5	mb	43	70	7.2	0.96	us	usc000hvve	1.37175E+12
20	2013-06-20T07:26:52.640+00:00	48.577	153.242	146.3	4.6	mb	68	127	5.3	0.6	us	usc000hvv8	1.37174E+12
21	2013-06-20T07:16:47.000+00:00	62.823	-149.473	57.9	3.2	Ml				0.81	ak	ak10742516	1.37174E+12
22	2013-06-20T06:27:56.500+00:00	19.146	-65.104	98	3	Md	6	284	0.8	0.31	pr	pr13171001	1.37171E+12
23	2013-06-20T06:00:31.820+00:00	52.396	159.556	35.1	4.7	mb	43	161	0.8	0.55	us	usc000hvuz	1.37174E+12
24	2013-06-20T03:45:39.300+00:00	35.925	-120.478	10.2	3	Md		32	0	0.1	nc	nc72011795	1.37177E+12

Figure 3-14. *Sample earthquake data*

1. Start a new Microsoft Visual Studio 2012 Console Application project. We have named our project readGeospatialDataToSQL.

2. You will now need a class to hold all of the earthquake data. We create the class Earthquake.cs that appears as follows:

```
using System;
using Microsoft.Maps.MapControl.WPF;

namespace readGeospatialDataToSQL
{
    public class Earthquake
    {
        public DateTime When { get; set; }
        public Location Location { get; set; }
        public float Depth { get; set; }
        public float Magnitude { get; set; }
        public string MagType { get; set; }
        public int NbStation { get; set; }
        public int Gap { get; set; }
        public float Distance { get; set; }
        public float RMS { get; set; }
        public string Source { get; set; }
        public string EventID { get; set; }
        public float Version { get; set; }
        public string Title { get; set; }
        public string Description { get; set; }
```

```
        public Earthquake(DateTime when, Location where, float depth, float magnitude,
string magType,
            int nbStation, int gap, float distance, float rms, string source, string eventId,
float version,
            string title, string description = "")

        {
            When = when;
            Location = where;
            Depth = depth;
            Magnitude = magnitude;
            MagType = magType;
            NbStation = nbStation;
            Gap = gap;
            Distance = distance;
            RMS = rms;
            Source = source;
            EventID = eventId;
            Version = version;
            Title = title;
            Description = description;
        }
    }
}
```

3. Additionally you will require a CVS file reader, CVSFileReader.cs. You can find one at
    http://www.blackbeltcoder.com/Articles/files/reading-and-writing-csv-files-in-c.
    We have refactored the code to only contain the reader, as we do not need a CVS writer for
    this sample.

4. Now you are ready to write the code to read in the CVS earthquake data file
    into the Earthquake object: private static List<Earthquake> _data
    = new List<Earthquake>(); that is a member of the class containing the
    GetRecentEarthquakes() method.

```
        public static void GetRecentEarthquakes()
        {

            WebClient client = new WebClient();
            Uri quakeDataURL = new Uri("http://earthquake.usgs.gov/earthquakes/feed/v0.1/
summary/2.5_day.csv");
            string quakeDataFile = "quake.csv";
            client.DownloadFile(quakeDataURL, quakeDataFile);
            CSVFileReader reader = new CSVFileReader(quakeDataFile);
            List<string> columns = new List<String>();
            bool readHeader = false;
            while (reader.ReadRow(columns))
            {
                Debug.Assert(true);
                if (readHeader)
                {
```

```
                          DateTime when = DateTime.Parse(columns[0]);
                          double lat = Convert.ToDouble(columns[1]);
                          double lon = Convert.ToDouble(columns[2]);
                          Location where = new Location(lat, lon);
                          float depth = columns[3] != "" ? Convert.ToSingle(columns[3]) : 0.0f;
                          float magnitude = columns[4] != "" ? Convert.ToSingle(columns[4]) : 0.0f;
                          string magType = columns[5];
                          int nbStation = columns[6] != "" ? Convert.ToInt16(columns[6]) : 0;
                          int gap = columns[7] != "" ? Convert.ToInt16(columns[7]) : 0;
                          float distance = columns[8] != "" ? Convert.ToSingle(columns[8]) : 0.0f;
                          float rms = columns[9] != "" ? Convert.ToSingle(columns[9]) : 0.0f;
                          string source = columns[10];
                          string eventId = columns[11];
                          float version = columns[12] != "" ? Convert.ToSingle(columns[12]) : 0.0f;
                          _data.Add(new Earthquake(when,
                                                   where,
                                                   depth,
                                                   magnitude,
                                                   magType,
                                                   nbStation,
                                                   gap,
                                                   distance,
                                                   rms,
                                                   source,
                                                   eventId,
                                                   version,
                                                   "M " + columns[4]));
                      }
                      else
                      {
                          readHeader = true;
                      }
                  }
              }
```

5. Finally, you can write the code to read the earthquake data into the SQL database. Earlier, we showed you how to create a table through the management portal. Here we will show you how to create the table programmatically. The SQL server login and password you created earlier will be useful. The username is a combination of the login and the server in the format <loginname>@<servername>, for example is myLogin and your server is myServername then your username will be myLogin@myServername.

It is good to note that the DateTime field is inserted into the SQL Database using a parameter @value. This abstraction is necessary due to the fact that DateTime types require single quotes around them to be inserted, for example '20130107', however, it can be often confused with a string.

Another interesting type is the geometry type, which is one of the geospatial types supported by SQL Database, as we described earlier. Here we used a single geometry, Point, to represent our latitude and longitude.

```
public static void insertQuakeDataToSQL()
    {
        // Provide the following information
        string userName = myLogin@myServername;
        string password = myPassword;
        string dataSource = "myServername.database.windows.net";
        string sampleDatabaseName = "EarthquakeMap";

        // Create a connection string for the sample database
        SqlConnectionStringBuilder connString2Builder;
        connString2Builder = new SqlConnectionStringBuilder();
        connString2Builder.DataSource = dataSource;
        connString2Builder.InitialCatalog = sampleDatabaseName;
        connString2Builder.Encrypt = true;
        connString2Builder.TrustServerCertificate = false;
        connString2Builder.UserID = userName;
        connString2Builder.Password = password;

        // Connect to the sample database and perform various operations
        using (SqlConnection conn = new SqlConnection(connString2Builder.ToString()))
        {
            string tableName = "earthquakeData";

            SqlCommand cmd = conn.CreateCommand();
            conn.Open();

            // Create a table
            cmd.CommandText = "CREATE TABLE " + tableName + "(" +
                                "DateTime datetime primary key," +
                                "Position geography," +
                                "Depth float," +
                                "Magnitude float," +
                                "MagType varchar(20)," +
                                "NbStation int," +
                                "Gap int," +
                                "Distance float," +
                                "RMS float," +
                                "Source varchar(20)," +
                                "EventID varchar(20)," +
                                "Version float," +
                                "Title varchar(20)," +
                                "Description varchar(30))";
            cmd.ExecuteNonQuery();

            string columnsToInsert = "INSERT INTO " + tableName + "(" +
                                "DateTime," +
                                "Position," +
                                "Depth," +
                                "Magnitude," +
```

```
                                    "MagType," +
                                    "NbStation," +
                                    "Gap," +
                                    "Distance," +
                                    "RMS," +
                                    "Source," +
                                    "EventID," +
                                    "Version," +
                                    "Title)";

            // INSERT data into SQL database
            foreach (var line in _data)
            {
                cmd = conn.CreateCommand();
                string valuesToInsert = " VALUES (" +
                                    "@value," +
                                    "geography::Point(" + line.Location.Latitude + "," +
                                    line.Location.Latitude + ", 4326), " +
                                    line.Depth + "," +
                                    line.Magnitude + ",'" +
                                    line.MagType + "'," +
                                    line.NbStation + ", " +
                                    line.Gap + ", " +
                                    line.Distance + ", " +
                                    line.RMS + ", '" +
                                    line.Source + "', '" +
                                    line.EventID + "', " +
                                    line.Version + ", '" +
                                    line.Title + "')";
                string commandString = columnsToInsert + valuesToInsert;
                cmd.CommandText = commandString;
                cmd.Parameters.AddWithValue("@value", line.When);
                cmd.ExecuteNonQuery();
                cmd.Dispose();
            }

            conn.Close();
        }
    }
```

Wrapping up

In this chapter you learned about hosting geospatial data on SQL Database. As you probably noted, transitioning from SQL Server to SQL Database is straightforward. One nice difference is the availability of the management portal. On the portal, you can create, manage, and delete databases. Of course, as an alternative to the management portal, you can still do many of the tasks, such as creating tables programmatically, rather than on the portal.

In our sample code in this chapter, we pulled geospatial data from the government earthquake site http://on.doi.gov/1cXCj1C. We inserted the code into an Earthquake class, and then inserted this data into our SQL database that we created in this chapter. In the following chapter, you will learn about WCF and how we can use it to provide a service that queries the database for client applications.

■ ■ ■

CHAPTER 4

Hosting WCF Services on Windows Azure

In Chapter 3 we showed you how to import your geospatial data onto an Azure SQL Database. In this chapter we will show you how to create and host WCF (Windows Communication Foundation) Services on Windows Azure that will serve your geospatial data to a client application. In the following section, we will give you a quick crash course about WCF. For a deeper understanding of it, we recommend a dedicated WCF book such as *Pro WCF4: Practical Microsoft SOA Implementation* by Nishith Pathak.

WCF: A Crash Course

WCF is a framework for developing and deploying service-oriented applications. These services are loosely coupled, provide some functionality, and have no internal calls to one another. Using WCF, data can be sent asynchronously between service endpoints. Together a group of services will provide the complete functionality of an entire software application. For example, if building an ATM machine software, one service could handle the login, another display the balance, and another counts and subtracts. These services provide the total functionality for the ATM machine software. This type of service-oriented design principle is known as Service Oriented Architecture (SOA). SOA is the architecture on which WCF is built. We will now describe the services and how they communicate.

Services

SOA allows for distributed computing such that services need not be co-located. Moreover, services can have multiple parties using them and can execute on different timelines. Services can even be version independent.

Clients consume the functionality of the service. Examples of clients can be WPF, a Windows Form, or even an ASP.NET webpage. The client and service communicate by sending messages back and forth. The service exposes metadata describing the functionality of the service and also how clients should communicate with it. The client then communicates indirectly with the service using a proxy. A client's proxy can communicate with one or more services' endpoints. As you see in Figure 4-1, there are two locations, perhaps "Location 1" is local and "Location 2" is remote. Machine 2 is running a client and can communicate with the service that is running on Machine 1 via the client proxy. Likewise, Machine 4 has a client whose proxy is communicating with the service running on Machine 3. Additionally, Machine 4's client is also communicating with Machine 1's service via the Internet. In the example in Figure 4.1, we see that a client can communicate with a service remotely but also that it can communicate with more than one service. Since the client uses proxies, the programming model is simplified as all types of clients, regardless of location, require the use of a proxy.

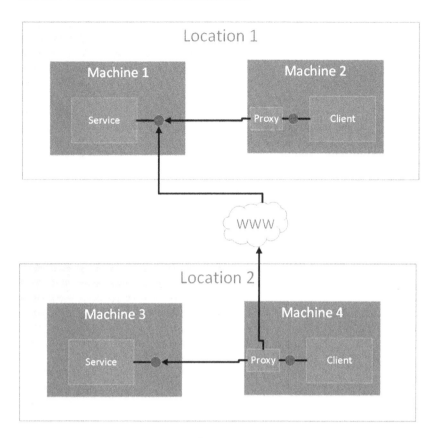

Figure 4-1. *WCF communication. Clients communicate with services via a proxy*

In Figure 4-1, there are also purple circles that represent endpoints. The endpoints contain addresses, bindings, and contracts, which conveniently can be abbreviated to ABC. We will describe the ABCs of endpoints subsequently.

Endpoints

The endpoint is comprised of the fusion of three parts: addresses, bindings, and contracts, as shown in Figure 4-2. Each endpoint must contain all three parts. Every service must expose at least one endpoint; however it can have multiple endpoints. These endpoints can use the same or different bindings and can have the same or different contracts. There is no relationship between these endpoints.

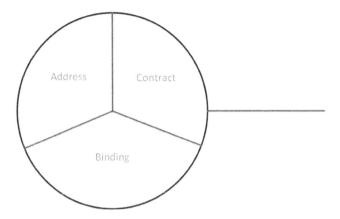

Figure 4-2. *Endpoints*

Addresses

In WCF, every service has a unique address with the following format: [base address]/[optional URI], where the base address looks like: [transport scheme]://[machine or domain][:optional port].

- A transport scheme is any one of the following supported schemes:
    - HTTP/HTTPS
    - TCP
    - IPC
    - Peer network
    - MSMQ
    - Service bus

An example service address would be *http://localhost:8000* or *net.tcp//localhost:8002/myservice*.

Bindings

The binding is what specifies how the data will be transferred by specifying the communication protocol. The first aspect of data transfer to consider is the method of transport. Above we have listed some of the supported transport protocols (HTTP, TCP, etc.). In addition to the different transport protocols, there are different options for encoding that message. For example, you can choose to leave the message as plain text, or you can use a binary encoding, or for larger payloads you can use Message Transport Optimization Mechanism (MTOM). There are also different options for message authentication from which to choose. As the message delivery may not always be reliable, it is important that the message be authenticated. Other choices are the type of security, the transaction propagation, and the interoperability. As you can see, there are potentially tens of thousands of permutations you can choose from simply to transfer your messages. WCF simplifies your choices by grouping together sets of communications that include your transport protocol, your message encoding, and your message authentication into pre-defined bindings. The binding, therefore, is a consistent pre-defined set of choices for your message communication.

Here are some common bindings:

- **Basic binding:** which basically looks like a legacy web service that communicates over the basic web service profile.

- **TCP binding:** uses TCP for communication over the intranet

- **IPC binding:** for same-machine communication

- **Web Service binding:** uses HTTP or HTTPS for transport over the Internet

- **MSMQ binding:** Binding used for disconnected queued calls.

Which binding you choose is largely an architectural decision. For example, a web service supporting external clients running in web browsers would likely choose the web service binding; a dedicated client-server all running in C# might use TCP binding because it's lower overhead, or web service binding to permit other web clients access over the lifespan of the application. When in doubt, the web service binding is a logical choice.

Contracts

Services expose **contracts** that describe what the service does via an **endpoint**. There are different types of contracts defined by WCF:

- **Service contracts:** Describe what operations can be performed by the client on the service.

- **Data contracts:** Describes what type of data are passed to and from the service. While **int** and **string** are the two pre-defined types, you can also define some custom types.

- **Fault contracts:** Define which errors are raised by the service and how the service handles the errors.

- **Message contracts**: Allows the service to interact directly with the message.

An example of an endpoint can be as follows:

```
<system.serviceModel>
  <services>
    <service name = "MyNamespace.MyService">
      <endpoint
        address = "http://localhost:8000/MyService"
        binding = "wsHttpBinding"
        contract = "MyNamespace.IMyContract"
      />
    </service>
  </services>
</system.serviceModel>
```

You can have multiple endpoints for the same service, and that will look as follows:

```
<system.serviceModel>
  <services>
    <service name = "MyNamespace.MyService">
      <endpoint
        address = "http://localhost:8000/MyService"
        binding = "wsHttpBinding"
        contract = "MyNamespace.IMyContract"
      />
```

```
    <endpoint
      address = "net.tcp://localhost:8002/MyService"
      binding = "NetTcpBinding"
      contract = "MyNamespace.IMyContract"
    />
    <endpoint
      address = "net.msmq://localhost/private/MyQueue"
      binding = "NetMsmqBinding"
      contract = "MyNamespace.IMyOtherContract"
    />
  </service>
 </services>
</system.serviceModel>
```

Alternatively, you can just rely on WCF to add the default endpoints to the services and not provide the endpoint specifications. For example, if using HTTP, WCF will use the basic binding.

Hosting

One additional aspect to discuss is the concept of hosting. Every WCF service is hosted in a Windows process called the host process, which can host multiple services. Moreover, a single service can be hosted by multiple processes. The host can be provided by Internet Information Services (IIS), Windows Activation Service (WAS), or, more recently, by Windows Server AppFabric. The host can also be provided by the developer as part of the application. Windows Server AppFabric provides additional configuration options, monitoring, instrumentation, and event tracking for both WCF services and Workflow services. It allows the services to auto-start without requiring the first client request. A service host will look as follows:

```
ServiceHost host = new ServiceHost(typeof(MyService),
  httpBaseAddress,
  tcpBaseAddress,
  icpBaseAddress);
host.Open();
```

WCF Client

A WCF Client application uses the WCF Client Proxy to communicate with the service. The application imports the services' metadata to generate the necessary code that can be used to invoke the service. The client first must compile the service code, then it must generate the WCF client proxy and finally it must instantiate the WCF client proxy. After which, the client is able to use the service.

WCF Client Proxy

The client proxy can be generated using Visual Studio by using the **Add Service Reference** option (right-click the project in the Solution Explorer). Alternatively it can be generated by using Service Model Metadata Utility Tool, which is a command line tool for generating code from metadata.

WCF Service for Earthquake Data

In this section we will show you how to build a WCF service that enables a client application to query the database for the earthquake data we loaded into Azure SQL Database in Chapter 3. We will then show you how you can host this service on Azure and finally how to write a client application that calls the service.

Creating the WCF Service

1. Launch Visual Studio 2012 and run as administrator. To run as administrator, you will right-click the application and select "Run as Administrator".

2. In the menu, start a new project by selecting File ➤ New ➤ Project.

3. Under **Templates**, select **Visual C#** and then **Cloud**, and select **Windows Azure Cloud Service** (It is likely the only choice on the list). We named our project **WCFEarthquakeService.** Click OK.

4. In the resulting New Windows Azure Cloud Service window, select from the Visual C# .NET Framework roles the WCF Service Web Role, and click ➤ to add the role to the Windows Azure Cloud Service solution. Click OK. Visual Studio will create the solution.

5. Select IService.cs to modify it with the desired interface to your service. In our case, you will add the following code listing:

   Listing 4-1. IService.cs. Service Interface for the WCF Service

   ```
   using System;
   using System.Collections.Generic;
   using System.ServiceModel;

   namespace WCFServiceWebRole1
   {
       [ServiceContract]
       public interface IService1
       {

           [OperationContract]
           List<Earthquake> GetEarthquakeData();

           [OperationContract]
           List<Earthquake> GetEarthquakeDataBBox(double TLLong, double TLLat,
             double BRLong, double BRLat);
       }
   }
   ```

You will note that in Listing 4-1 there are two methods declared, each method has the declaration [OperationContract] that precedes it to indicate that the method defines an operation that is part of a service contract for a WCF application. Both methods will retrieve earthquake data from the Azure SQL Database, the first will return all earthquake data in the database, and the second, GetEarthquakeDataBBox will return the earthquake data that is within a given bounding box. The bounding box is defined by the longitude and latitude of the top-left corner of the bounding box (TLLong, TLLat) and the longitude and latitude of the bottom-right corner of the bounding box (BRLong and BRLat).

Both methods return a list of Earthquake objects as defined in Earthquake.cs in Chapter 3. You will need to modify this class in order to be part of the service contract. As you can see in Listing 4-2, the class is defined as part of the data contract and each member of the class is defined to be a data member.

■ **Note**   Don't forget to add the MapControl reference in order to be able to use the Location type.

Listing 4-2. Earthquake.cs. Each member must be explicitly defined as a data member

```
using System;
using System.Runtime.Serialization;
using Microsoft.Maps.MapControl.WPF;

namespace WCFServiceWebRole1
{
    [DataContract]
    public class Earthquake
    {
        [DataMember]
        public DateTime When { get; set; }
        [DataMember]
        public Location Location { get; set; }
        [DataMember]
        public float Depth { get; set; }
        [DataMember]
        public float Magnitude { get; set; }
        [DataMember]
        public string MagType { get; set; }
        [DataMember]
        public int NbStation { get; set; }
        [DataMember]
        public int Gap { get; set; }
        [DataMember]
        public float Distance { get; set; }
        [DataMember]
        public float RMS { get; set; }
        [DataMember]
        public string Source { get; set; }
        [DataMember]
        public string EventID { get; set; }
        [DataMember]
        public float Version { get; set; }
        [DataMember]
        public string Title { get; set; }
        [DataMember]
        public string Description { get; set; }
```

```
public Earthquake(DateTime when, Location where,
    float depth, float magnitude, string magType,
    int nbStation, int gap, float distance, float rms,
    string source, string eventId, float version,
      string title, string description = "")
{
    When = when;
    Location = where;
    Depth = depth;
    Magnitude = magnitude;
    MagType = magType;
    NbStation = nbStation;
    Gap = gap;
    Distance = distance;
    RMS = rms;
    Source = source;
    EventID = eventId;
    Version = version;
    Title = title;
    Description = description;
}
}
}
```

6. Next we will modify the Service1.svc.cs, which contains the implementation of the two methods declared in the service interface, IService.cs. To implement GetEarthquakeData(), you will query the database for all the earthquakes with the following query string:

    SELECT <desired fields> FROM <my SQL table name>.

    In our case it will be:

    SELECT DateTime, Position, Magnitude, Depth, MagType, NbStation, Gap, Distance, RMS, Source, EventID, Version, Title FROM earthquakeData

The full listing for this method is in Listing 4-3.

Listing 4-3. Method to create query string to request all earthquakes from the SQL database

```
public List<Earthquake> GetEarthquakeData()
{
  string tableName = "earthquakeData";
    var queryString = "SELECT DateTime, " +
      "Position, " +
      "Magnitude, " +
      "Depth, " +
      "MagType, " +
      "NbStation, " +
      "Gap, " +
      "Distance, " +
```

```
        "RMS, " +
        "Source, " +
        "EventID, " +
        "Version, " +
        "Title FROM " + tableName;
    return GetEarthquakesFromSql(queryString);
}
```

Clearly there is an important part of the code that has been abstracted away, which you will find in the method GetEarthquakesFromSql. First you will create the connection to the database as you did in Chapter 3. You will use the same credentials as you did in Chapter 3, and you should also be using the same server, database, and table as in Chapter 3, if you want to retrieve the same earthquake data you fetched in the earlier example.

Once you have retrieved the data, you will need to parse this data into the Earthquake class and append to the list of Earthquakes we have defined as data. For the most part, parsing the data is straightforward, particularly when retrieving common types such as string and int. You must simply cast the SQL objects to the correct types. You will note the odd double cast for magnitude and other data that was stored as float types in SQL. For some reason, a float in SQL Server is retrieved to type double of .NET, so you will need to cast to double and then cast back to float. Lastly, we look at how to parse the geography data. When the SQL reader receives the geography data from the SQL Database, the type of this data is not yet known to the reader. Thus, a direct cast is not possible. The workaround for this issue is to read the data into a byte array and then cast to the SQLGeography type. From there, you can convert this data into the Location type from the MapControl that the Earthquake object expects for Location data.

In order to use the SQLGeography type, you will need to include a reference to the SqlServer.Types. You can usually find this library where you have your SQL Server libraries on your machine. In our case it was in C:\Program Files (x86)\Microsoft SQL Server\110\SDK\Assemblies.

■ **Note** In order for the references to be included in the package you will be creating for Azure, right-click on the reference, and select Properties. Under Copy Local, you should make sure it is **True**. Leaving the property to be False will result in the reference not being copied to the output directory, and therefore not included in the service package you will deploy to Azure.

The namespaces you will need to include are also listed in Listing 4-4.

Listing 4-4. Method to query the Azure SQL Database for the earthquake data

```
using System;
using System.Collections.Generic;
using System.Data.SqlClient;
using Microsoft.Maps.MapControl.WPF;
using Microsoft.SqlServer.Types;

public List<Earthquake> GetEarthquakesFromSql(String queryString)
{
  // Provide the following information
  string userName = <my Azure SQL Database username>;
  string password = <my Azure SQL Database password> ;
  string dataSource = <my Azure SQL Server name>
  string sampleDatabaseName = <my Azure SQL Database name>;
```

```csharp
// Create a connection string for the sample database
SqlConnectionStringBuilder connString2Builder;
connString2Builder = new SqlConnectionStringBuilder();
connString2Builder.DataSource = dataSource;
connString2Builder.InitialCatalog = sampleDatabaseName;
connString2Builder.Encrypt = true;
connString2Builder.TrustServerCertificate = false;
connString2Builder.UserID = userName;
connString2Builder.Password = password;

// Connect to the sample database and perform various operations
using (SqlConnection conn = new SqlConnection(connString2Builder.ToString()))
{
  SqlCommand cmd = conn.CreateCommand();
  conn.Open();
  cmd.CommandText = queryString;

  var data = new List<Earthquake>();
  using (SqlDataReader reader = cmd.ExecuteReader())
  {
    while (reader.Read())
    {
      var when = (DateTime)reader.GetValue(0);
      var position = SqlGeography.Deserialize(reader.GetSqlBytes(1));
      var where = new Location((double)position.Lat, (double)position.Long);
      var magnitude = (float)(double)reader.GetValue(2);
      var depth = (float)(double)reader.GetValue(3);
      var magType = (string)reader.GetValue(4);
      var nbStation = (int)reader.GetValue(5);
      var gap = (int)reader.GetValue(6);
      var distance = (float)(double)reader.GetValue(7);
      var rms = (float)(double)reader.GetValue(8);
      var source = (string)reader.GetValue(9);
      var eventId = (string)reader.GetValue(10);
      var version = (float)(double)reader.GetValue(11);
      var title = (string)reader.GetValue(12);

      data.Add(new Earthquake(when,
        where,
        depth,
        magnitude,
        magType,
        nbStation,
        gap,
        distance,
        rms,
        source,
        eventId,
```

```
        version,
        title));
      }
    }

  conn.Close();

  return data;
  }
}
```

The implementation of GetEarthquakeDataBBox is essentially just as GetEarthquakeData, however, the query string will differ in that we will add a filter to the query that defines the bounding box and filters the data to only return the entries that lie within the bounding box. The query string will have the following format:

```
DECLARE @g geography; SET @g=geography::STGeomFromText('POLYGON((<my bounding box coordinates>))',
4326); SELECT <desired fields> FROM <my SQL database table name> WHERE <my geo data field>.
Filter(@g)=1"
```

Note how we're using the SQL extensions here: we create a POLYGON of our bounding coordinates and perform a geospatial query in our table.

In our case, we create the string as in Listing 4-5.

Listing 4-5. Request all the earthquake data from within a bounding box

```
public List<Earthquake> GetEarthquakeDataBBox(double TLLong, double TLLat,
  double BRLong, double BRLat)
{
  string tableName = "earthquakeData";
  var selectString = "SELECT DateTime, " +
    "Position, " +
    "Magnitude, " +
    "Depth, " +
    "MagType, " +
    "NbStation, " +
    "Gap, " +
    "Distance, " +
    "RMS, " +
    "Source, " +
    "EventID, " +
    "Version, " +
    "Title FROM " + tableName;

  string bboxString = "POLYGON((" +
    TLLong + " " + TLLat + ", " +
    BRLong + " " + TLLat + ", " +
    BRLong + " " + BRLat + ", " +
    TLLong + " " + BRLat + ", " +
    TLLong + " " + TLLat +
    "))";
  var setGeometry = "DECLARE @g geography; SET @g=geography::STGeomFromText('" +
    bboxString + "', 4326); ";
  var queryFilter = " WHERE Position.Filter(@g)=1";
```

```
  var queryString = setGeometry + selectString + queryFilter;
  return GetEarthquakesFromSql(queryString);
}
```

7. You have now created your WCF service and you can run it locally by selecting Debug ➤ Start Without Debugging. Visual Studio will launch the browser that will have your service running with a URL of `http://127.0.0.2:81/Service1.svc` (The port number may be different). Now the service is running locally.

Although not necessary for implementation, we would like to draw your attention to the `ServiceDefinition.csdef` file. This file contains all the service definitions we talked about at the beginning of the chapter. You will note the bindings and endpoints have all been automatically generated when you created your solution! You can also specify the virtual machine size in this file. The default is set to small, but you may want to set it to extra small while testing since the extra small VM has the lowest bill rate per usage.

Two other files were automatically generated: `ServiceConfiguration.Local.cscfg` and `ServiceConfiguration.Cloud.cscfg`. These files provide the configuration settings for your application, including the number of instances to run for each role. By default the instance count is set to 1. We will leave that instance number at 1 for our sample codes, but for robustness, you may want to run multiple instances of the same role when you deploy your own applications.

Hosting the WCF Service on Azure

1. You will need to publish the service package and service configuration package before you can deploy your service on Azure. Right-click on the WCFEarthquakeService project name in the Solution Explorer and select Package. A Package Windows Azure Application pop-up window will appear.

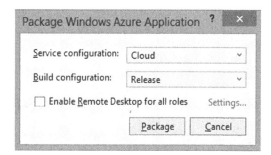

As you will be deploying to Azure, you can leave the Service configuration as Cloud. Click **Package**. Visual Studio will open a folder that contains your two files: **ServiceConfiguration.Cloud.cscfg** and **WCFEarthquakeService.cspkg**, which are the configuration files and service package respectively. Take note of where these files are saved as you will need them later.

2. Log in to your management portal for Windows Azure at **windowsazure.com**. You can click on **Portal** at the top of the page. Or you can get there directly by going to **http://manage.windowsazure.com**.

3. Select New at the bottom of the page in order to create a new service.

4. Create a new custom Cloud Service. Note, you may find that some sites refer to this as a Hosted Service.

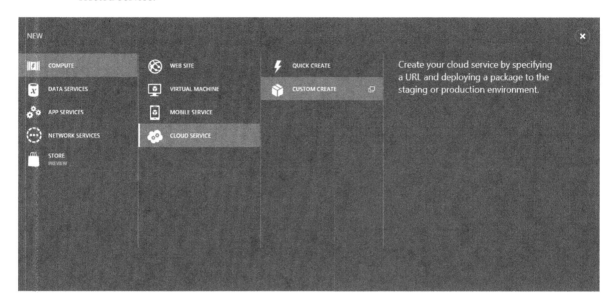

5. You will be asked to give a URL name to the service. We chose **myEarthquakeService**. Click Next.

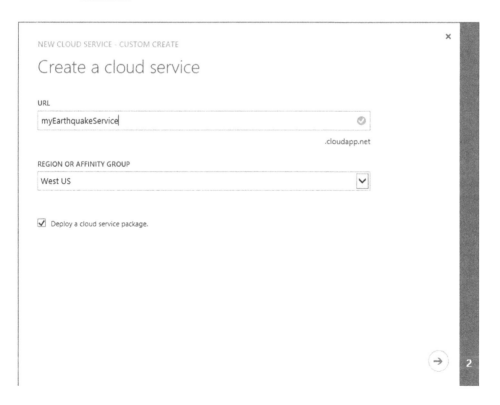

6. You can enter a deployment name for the service. It is here that you will upload the packages generated in Step 1. You can choose to deploy to the Staging or Production environment. We have chosen Staging. Finally, recall that the default of the Service you created was a single instance of the webrole. If you did not change the number of instances to more than 1, then you will need to check **Deploy even if one or more roles contain a single instance** in order for your deployment to work. Click the check mark to create your cloud service. It may take a few minutes to finish the deployment.

NEW CLOUD SERVICE - CUSTOM CREATE

Publish your cloud service

This will create a new **staging** deployment.

DEPLOYMENT NAME

EarthquakeServiceName

PACKAGE

WCFEarthquakeService.cspkg   ■ FROM LOCAL   ▦ FROM STORAGE

CONFIGURATION

ServiceConfiguration.Cloud.cscfg   ■ FROM LOCAL   ▦ FROM STORAGE

ENVIRONMENT

PRODUCTION   STAGING

☑ Deploy even if one or more roles contain a single instance. ⦾

☑ Start deployment

☐ Add certificates

7. Once the service has been successfully created, you can click on the newly created service, **myEarthquakeService**, in the management portal to see more details. As we have chosen to deploy to the Staging environment, click on **Staging**. If you scroll down the page, you will see a list of the details pertaining to this service. The status will be set to Running. It is also here that you will see the URL for the deployed service. It will be listed under Site URL, and be in the form: `http://<guid>.cloudapp.net`. If you click on the link you will be brought to that page. From there you will be able to select your service, Service1.svc, so that you will now have your service open in the browser at: `http://<guid>.cloudapp.net/Service1.svc`. Take note of this URL you will be calling it in your client application. Your WCF service is now running in Azure! If you deployed to **Production** rather than **Staging** then the URL will be `http://<URLname>.cloudapp.net/Service1.svc`.

Client Application

There are a variety of client applications that can call this WCF service. We will show you how to build one simple client application that runs locally on your machine.

1. Open Visual Studio and create a new project: File ➤ New ➤ Project. Under Template ➤ Visual C# ➤ Windows select **Console Application**. Name your application. We named ours getEarthquakeDataApp. Click **OK**.

2. In the Solution Explorer, right-click the project name and select **Add Service Reference**.

3. In the resulting pop-up window, in the **Address** textbox, enter the URL of your Azure-deployed WCF Service and click **Go**. (If you are running the service locally, then add that URL instead.) Your service will appear under **Services**. Click on **Advanced**. Recall that when you created your service, the service was returning a list of earthquakes. Change the Collection Type to **System.Collections.Generic.List**. Click **Ok**. Click **Ok** to add the Service Reference.

■ **Note**   You can always change the Service Reference configuration by right-clicking the service reference and selecting Configure Service Reference. If you make changes to the WCF Service, do not forget to update your service by right-clicking on the service reference and selecting Update Service Reference.

---

4. Modify the Program.cs file to call your service. Our program is quite simple. It will first request all the earthquakes in the database from the WCF service, and then request all the earthquakes within a bounding box from the service, see the code in Listing 4-6. You will need to include the service reference and then create an instance of this service client. Once you've done so, you can use this service client object to call the methods in your WCF service. In our case they will be GetEarthquakeData and GetEarthquakeDataBBox. You will need to include the Earthquake class from Listing 4-2, without the data contracts. The class can also be found in Chapter 3 in the sample code.

Listing 4-6. Client Application to call the WCF Service

```
using System;
using System.Collections.Generic;
using getEarthquakeDataApp.ServiceReference1;

namespace getEarthquakeDataApp
{
    class Program
    {
        static void Main(string[] args)
        {
            Service1Client client = null;

            try
            {
                client = new Service1Client();
                var test = client.GetEarthquakeData();
                var data = new List<Earthquake>();
```

```
            foreach (var earthquake in test)
            {
                var when = earthquake.When;
                var where = earthquake.Location;
                var magnitude = earthquake.Magnitude;
                var depth = earthquake.Depth;
                var magType = earthquake.MagType;
                var nbStation = earthquake.NbStation;
                var gap = earthquake.Gap;
                var distance = earthquake.Distance;
                var rms = earthquake.RMS;
                var source = earthquake.Source;
                var eventId = earthquake.EventID;
                var version = earthquake.Version;
                var title = earthquake.Title;
                Console.WriteLine("{0}, {1}, {2}, {3}, {4}, {5}, {6}, {7}, {8}, {9}, {10}, {11},
{12}", when, where, magnitude, depth, magType, nbStation, gap, distance, rms, source, eventId,
version, title);
                data.Add(new Earthquake(when, where, magnitude, depth, magType, nbStation, gap,
distance, rms, source, eventId, version, title));
            }

            var test2 = client.GetEarthquakeDataBBox(-145, 0, -75, 45);
            var data2 = new List<Earthquake>();
            foreach (var earthquake in test2)
            {
                var when = earthquake.When;
                var where = earthquake.Location;
                var magnitude = earthquake.Magnitude;
                var depth = earthquake.Depth;
                var magType = earthquake.MagType;
                var nbStation = earthquake.NbStation;
                var gap = earthquake.Gap;
                var distance = earthquake.Distance;
                var rms = earthquake.RMS;
                var source = earthquake.Source;
                var eventId = earthquake.EventID;
                var version = earthquake.Version;
                var title = earthquake.Title;
                Console.WriteLine("{0}, {1}, {2}, {3}, {4}, {5}, {6}, {7}, {8}, {9}, {10}, {11},
{12}", when, where, magnitude, depth, magType, nbStation, gap, distance, rms, source, eventId,
version, title);
                data2.Add(new Earthquake(when, where, magnitude, depth, magType, nbStation, gap,
distance, rms, source, eventId, version, title));
            }
        }
        catch (Exception e)
        {
            Console.WriteLine("Exception encounter: {0}", e.Message);
        }
        finally
```

```
        {
            Console.WriteLine("Done!");
            if (null != client)
            {
                client.Close();
            }
        }
    }
  }
}
```

A Note on Debugging:

The majority of your debugging as you develop would be conveniently done if you run the service locally first. This will avoid having to deploy to Azure every time you make a slight change. It also ensures that you are not paying while you are developing and not actually needing the service to be up and running. Debugging a service that is deployed on Azure requires some setup.

1. To be able to see why your Azure service cannot run, you will need to add the following to your web.config file:

```
<system.web>
  <customErrors mode="Off"/>
</system.web>
```

The element **customErrors** indicates whether filtered or complete exception information is returned by the server. There are three options for mode: **Off**, **On,** and **RemoteOnly**. The default is RemoteOnly, which returns complete exception information only to callers on the same machine. Setting **customError** to **Off** allows you to see the exceptions when your Azure-deployed service fails to run. When you click on the URL of the service, the browser will show you the exceptions rather than the running service.

2. If your service runs, when your client calls the service, there may still be errors within the service that you did not catch when debugging locally. You will want the client to be able to see these exceptions. In order to do so, you will need to turn the includeExceptionDetailInFaults on in your web.config file:

```
<behavior name="metadataAndDebugEnabled">
  <serviceDebug
    includeExceptionDetailInFaults="true"
  />
  <serviceMetadata
    httpGetEnabled="true"
    httpGetUrl=""
  />
</behavior>
```

Additionally, in Service1.svc.cs, you will add the following before you implement the service methods:

```
[ServiceBehavior(
    IncludeExceptionDetailInFaults = true
  )]
```

Setting `IncludeExceptionDetailInFaults` to `true` allows clients to obtain information internal service exceptions.

Wrapping Up

In this chapter you learned how to create a WCF service that serves geospatial data from an Azure SQL Database to clients. You then learned how to host that service on Azure and create a client application that calls the service. WCF may not be the only way to create service-oriented applications, but as you have seen in this chapter, it makes the development of such services straightforward and easy.

■ ■ ■

CHAPTER 5

Map Visualization with Bing Maps for the Web

We are now finally able to begin your first Bing map application with all the pieces you made in the previous chapters! In this chapter you will learn how to visualize the earthquake data we collected in Chapter 3, using the WCF data service developed in Chapter 4 on the Azure-hosted web-based Bing map created in Chapter 2.

We will begin this chapter by walking you through some of the basic Bing Maps API. In this book we are using the Bing Maps Ajax Control Version 7.0, which in conjunction with the Bing Maps REST services, provide you with the ability to create web-based Bing Maps applications. The extensive API for these controls are available at the MSDN website: http://bit.ly/1cCGT6R. There is also an interactive SDK online that provides template code for much of the functionality: http://bit.ly/1eAcEKz.

Bing Maps Ajax Control Basics

In Chapter 2, you learned how to display a basic web-based Bing map and host it on Windows Azure. Recall that in order to display the map, you will need your Bing Maps key, which you obtained in Chapter 2. You will then replace the string 'Your Bing Maps Key' in the following command with that key:

```
map = new Microsoft.Maps.Map(document.getElementById('SDKmap'),
    {credentials: 'Your Bing Maps Key'});
```

The resulting map will look like Figure 5-1. This basic map serves as a jumping off point to a variety of different map options and features. We will discuss a few of those options in the remainder of the chapter.

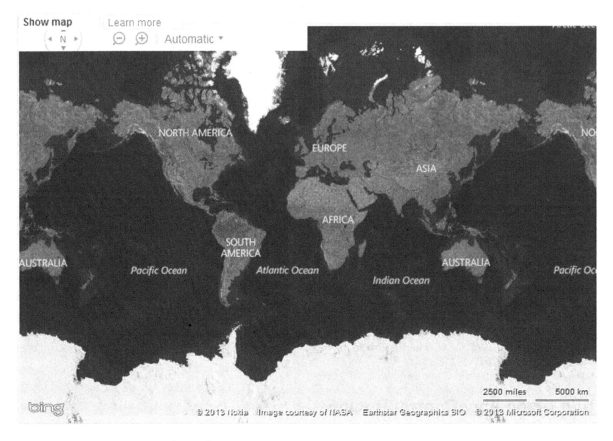

Figure 5-1. Basic Bing Map with map key

Playing with the map view

When the default map opens, it appears as in Figure 5-1. At times you may want the map to be centered at a different location. You can specify the map's center as follows:

```
map.setView({ center: new Microsoft.Maps.Location(47.6, -122.33) });
```

The map is now centered at a location somewhere near Seattle, USA but will remain at the same zoom level as in Figure 5-2.

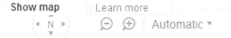

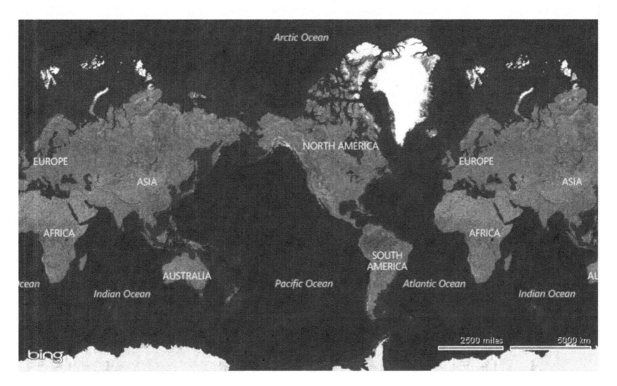

Figure 5-2. *Basic Bing map centered on Seattle, USA*

If we wanted to zoom in the map, we can change the zoom by setting the zoom level in the setView command:

```
map.setView({ center: new Microsoft.Maps.Location(47.6, -122.33), zoom: 10});
```

The map will now be zoomed in at the Seattle location at the level of zoom shown in Figure 5-3.

Figure 5-3. *Basic map zoomed in on Seattle location at zoom level 10*

Map Markers

The most common type of map marker is the basic pushpin. The basic pushpin can be added using the code listing in Listing 5-1. You will note that it is similar to the code for the basic map with the addition of the following commands:

```
var pushpin= new Microsoft.Maps.Pushpin(map.getCenter(), null);
map.entities.push(pushpin);
```

Listing 5-1. HTML code to insert a basic pushpin onto the Bing map

```
<!DOCTYPE html PUBLIC "-//W3C//DTD XHTML 1.0 Transitional//EN"
"http://www.w3.org/TR/xhtml1/DTD/xhtml1-transitional.dtd">
<html>
    <head>
        <title>Add default pushpin</title>
        <meta http-equiv="Content-Type" content="text/html; charset=utf-8"/>
        <script type="text/javascript" src="http://ecn.dev.virtualearth.net/mapcontrol/mapcontrol.
ashx?v=7.0"></script>
        <script type="text/javascript">
        var map = null;
```

```
    function getMap()
    {
      map = new Microsoft.Maps.Map(document.getElementById('myMap'),
        {credentials: 'Your Bing Maps Key'});
    }

    function addDefaultPushpin()
    {
      var pushpin= new Microsoft.Maps.Pushpin(map.getCenter(), null);
      map.entities.push(pushpin);
    }
    </script>
  </head>
  <body onload="getMap();">
    <div id='myMap' style="position:relative; width:400px; height:400px;"></div>
    <div>
        <input type="button" value="AddDefaultPushpin"
            onclick="addDefaultPushpin();" />
    </div>
  </body>
</html>
```

A pushpin is created with the location set to the map center. The newly created pushpin is then pushed onto the map as seen in Figure 5-4.

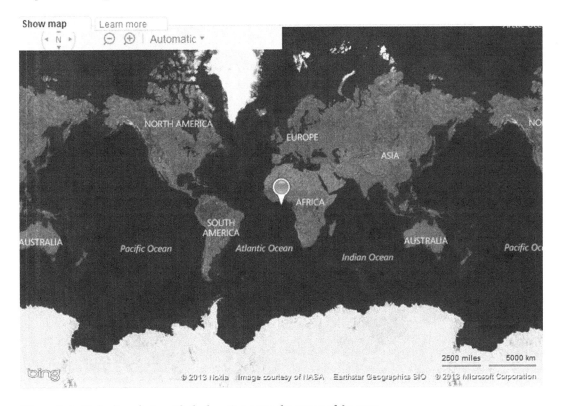

Figure 5-4. *Default pushpin with the location set to the center of the map*

Setting the location of a pushpin

If we wanted to specify the location of the pushpin to a location other than the center of the map, then we change the create pushpin command to:

```
var pushpin = new Microsoft.Maps.Pushpin(
  new Microsoft.Maps.Location(myLatitude, myLongitude),
  null);
```

The arguments myLatitude and myLongitude are replaced with the corresponding latitude and longitude of where you would like the pushpin to appear. You will notice that thus far, the Microsoft.Maps.Pushpin command takes two arguments, of which the second command we have left null. This is actually where we can put some additional pushpin options. A list of the options can be found here: http://bit.ly/1cnjU03. For example, you can set the pushpin visibility to true or false, or even specify the pushpin height and width. An example of some pushpin options is as follows:

```
var pushpinOptions = { text: 'hi', visible: true };
var pushpin = new Microsoft.Maps.Pushpin(
  new Microsoft.Maps.Location(myLatitude, myLongitude),
  pushpinOptions);
```

The option set is that the pushpin will place the string 'hi' in the pushpin, the visibility is set to true. It will look as in Figure 5-5.

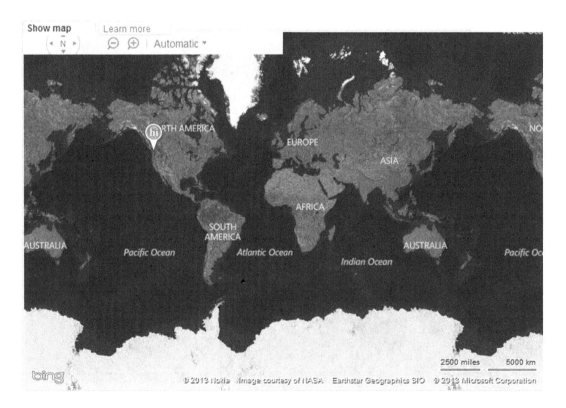

Figure 5-5. *Pushpin in Bing Map with a location set and the text option turned on and set to 'hi'*

Polygons

Another possible option for Bing maps is the ability to draw polygons on the map. The most basic polygon is a polyline. With the following code snippet we can draw a square around Union Square in San Francisco. We have also centered the map at Union Square and set the zoom level to 15 so the polyline is visible.

```
map.entities.clear();
var polyline = new Microsoft.Maps.Polyline(
  [
    new Microsoft.Maps.Location(37.788327,-122.408447),
    new Microsoft.Maps.Location(37.788531,-122.406837),
    new Microsoft.Maps.Location(37.787607,-122.406676),
    new Microsoft.Maps.Location(37.787412,-122.408264),
    new Microsoft.Maps.Location(37.788327,-122.408447)
  ], null);
map.setView( { center: new Microsoft.Maps.Location(37.788327,-122.408447), zoom:15});
map.entities.push(polyline);
```

The polyline is comprised of four latitude and longitude pairs, with the first point being repeated at the end in order to close the loop: (37.788327,-122.408447), (37.788531,-122.406837), (37.787607,-122.406676), (37.787412,-122.408264). The resulting map appears as in Figure 5-6.

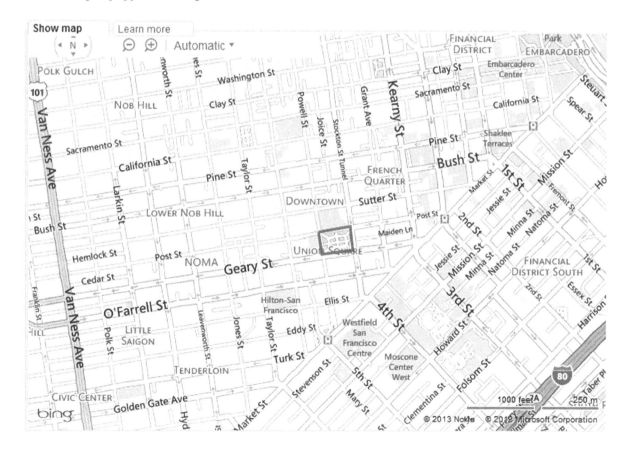

Figure 5-6. *Polyline drawn around Union Square in San Francisco*

If we wanted to draw a polygon instead, for example, we would use a polygon shape rather than a polyline. The code would change as follows:

```
map.entities.clear();
var polygon = new Microsoft.Maps.Polygon(
  [
    new Microsoft.Maps.Location(37.788327,-122.408447),
    new Microsoft.Maps.Location(37.788531,-122.406837),
    new Microsoft.Maps.Location(37.787607,-122.406676),
    new Microsoft.Maps.Location(37.787412,-122.408264),
    new Microsoft.Maps.Location(37.788327,-122.408447)
  ], null);
map.setView( { center: new Microsoft.Maps.Location(37.788327,-122.408447), zoom:15});
map.entities.push(polygon);
```

And the resulting polygon on the map will appear as in Figure 5-7. You'll note that because we have used the same location pairs, the shape remains the same as Figure 5-6, however, it is now shaded in. There are other options that you can apply to the polygons, such as adjusting the colors, opacity of the fill color, and line thickness, and we encourage you to see the API for more information on these options.

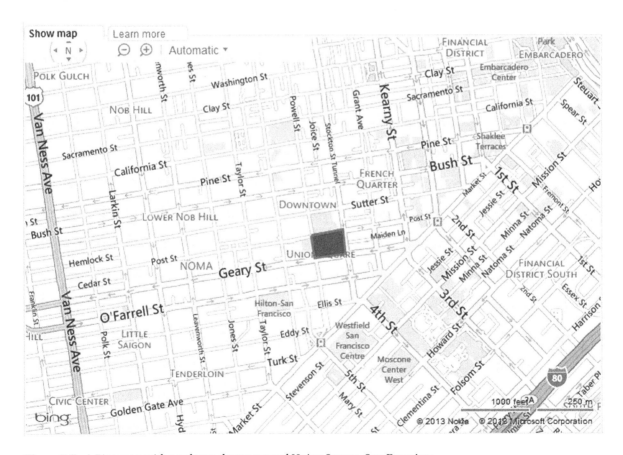

Figure 5-7. *A Bing map with a polygon drawn around Union Square, San Francisco*

Putting it all together

Now that we have learned some basic map options, we are ready to build our sample code for this chapter. In this sample application, we will be displaying the earthquake data that we retrieved in Chapter 3 on a web-based Bing map using pushpins.

Begin by setting up your solution:

1. Create an empty project in C# in Visual Studio (File > New Project). Under C# > Web, select **ASP.NET MVC 4 Web Application**.

2. Name this application **MvcEarthquakeMap** and click OK.

3. Select an Empty project template and the View engine to be Razor. Click OK and Visual Studio will have created all the dummy folders and files for your project.

You have now created a Model-View-Controller project. We will not be covering the specifics of MVC paradigms in this book; however, we will provide a simple explanation that pertains to our particular example. In Figure 5-8, we have drawn how our MVC is used.

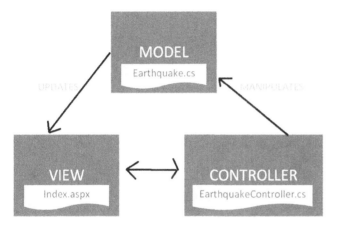

Figure 5-8. *The Model-View-Controller used in this sample application*

Create the Model

We begin with an Earthquake model. This model is a basic class that contains the data types that are required to represent an earthquake data. We have used this class in Chapter 3, and relist the code here for clarity in code Listing 5-2. Right-click on the folder Models in the Solution Explorer of Visual Studio and select Add>Class. Name this class **Earthquake.cs** and paste Listing 5-2 over the created class.

Listing 5-2. Earthquake.cs

```csharp
using System;
using Microsoft.Maps.MapControl.WPF;

namespace MvcEarthquakeMap.Models
{
    public class Earthquake
    {
        public DateTime When { get; set; }
        public Location Location { get; set; }
        public float Depth { get; set; }
        public float Magnitude { get; set; }
        public string MagType { get; set; }
        public int NbStation { get; set; }
        public int Gap { get; set; }
        public float Distance { get; set; }
        public float RMS { get; set; }
        public string Source { get; set; }
        public string EventID { get; set; }
        public float Version { get; set; }
        public string Title { get; set; }
        public string Description { get; set; }

        public Earthquake(DateTime when, Location where,
            float depth, float magnitude, string magType,
            int nbStation, int gap, float distance,
            float rms, string source, string eventId, float version,
            string title, string description = "")
        {
            When = when;
            Location = where;
            Depth = depth;
            Magnitude = magnitude;
            MagType = magType;
            NbStation = nbStation;
            Gap = gap;
            Distance = distance;
            RMS = rms;
            Source = source;
            EventID = eventId;
            Version = version;
            Title = title;
            Description = description;
        }
    }
}
```

You will need to add the `Microsoft.Maps.MapControl.WPF` reference by right-clicking References and selecting Add Reference.

Loading the Earthquake Data (The Controller)

Once the Earthquake model is created, you need to load the earthquake data into it. This step is done in the controller, which you create by right-clicking Controllers and selecting Add>Controller. Select the Empty Controller and name it **EarthquakeController.cs.** Once you select OK, the corresponding stub code will be created. You now need to add the namespace for the Earthquake model at the top of the page:

```
using MvcEarthquakeMap.Models;
```

In Chapter 4, we discussed how to create a WCF data service that pulled the earthquake data from the SQL Database. We will assume that this data loaded magically into a List called quakes in the function GetLocations():

```
public ActionResult Index()
{
    List<Earthquake> quakes = GetLocations();
    return View(quakes);
}
```

We then pass the data structure containing the Earthquake model to the View.

Displaying the Earthquake Data (The View)

To create the view, you can right-click on the Controller function:

```
Public ActionResult Index()
```

And select **Add View**. Leave the name as **Index**, select **ASPX** as the View engine, and **check Create a strongly-typed view**, and Earthquake (MvcEarthquakeMap.Models) as the Model class as in Figure 5-9. The strongly-typed view you selected will allow the Earthquake model to be visible from the newly created view.

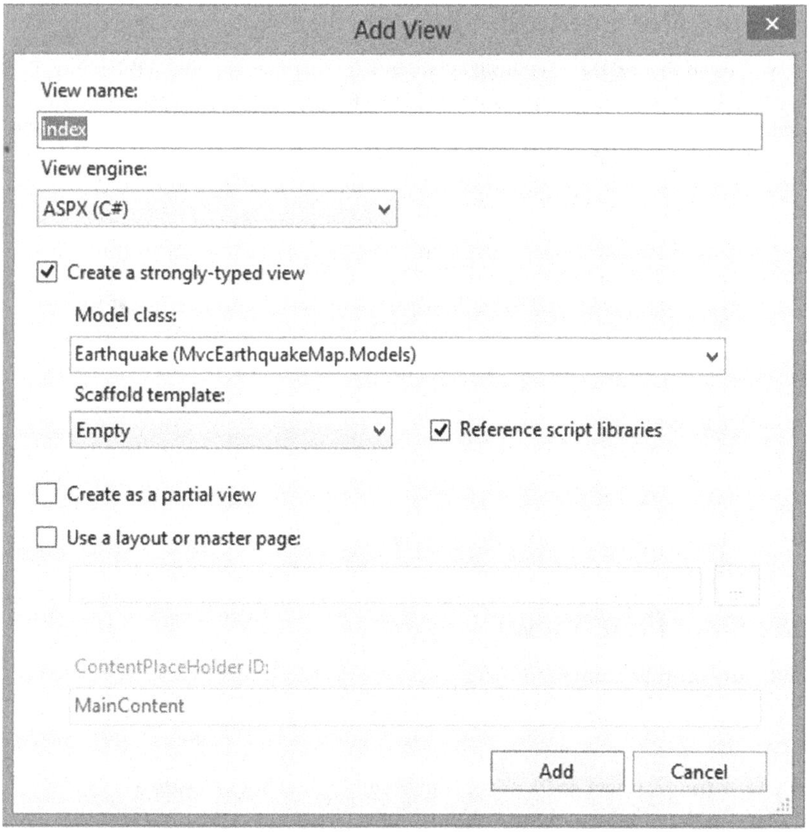

Figure 5-9. Create view form. Create a strongly-typed view so that the model will be visible from the view

Once you click **Add**, the stub code for the view will be created. At the top of Index.aspx, you will find the following line of code:

```
<%@ Page Language="C#" Inherits="System.Web.Mvc.ViewPage<MvcEarthquakeMap.Models.Earthquake>" %>
```

By including this, you have enabled the model to be visible in this view. You will remember, however, that we passed a list of the Earthquake models to the view, and not simply the Earthquake model alone. Thus, we change that code to reflect the list data structure:

```
<%@ Page Language="C#"
Inherits="System.Web.Mvc.ViewPage<List<MvcEarthquakeMap.Models.Earthquake>>" %>
```

Now the entire list of the model is visible in the view. Paste in Listing 5-3 into the Index.aspx.

Listing 5-3. Listing for the view that displays the Earthquake data in the map

```
<%@ Page Language="C#" Inherits="System.Web.Mvc.ViewPage<List<MvcEarthquakeMap.Models.Earthquake>>" %>
<!DOCTYPE html>

<html>
 <head>
     <title>Add default pushpin</title>
     <meta http-equiv="Content-Type" content="text/html; charset=utf-8"/>
     <script type="text/javascript"
src="http://ecn.dev.virtualearth.net/mapcontrol/mapcontrol.ashx?v=7.0"></script>

        <script type="text/javascript">
            var map = null;

            function getMap() {
                map = new Microsoft.Maps.Map(document.getElementById('myMap'),
                { credentials: 'your_bing_maps_credentials' });
            }

            function addPushpins() {
                var offset = new Microsoft.Maps.Point(0, 5);
                <% foreach (var item in Model)
                    {%>
                var pushpinOptions = { text: '<%=item.Magnitude%>',
                  visible: true, textOffset: offset };
                var pushpin = new Microsoft.Maps.Pushpin(
                  new Microsoft.Maps.Location(<%=item.Location.Longitude%>,
                    <%=item.Location.Latitude%>),
                    pushpinOptions);
                map.entities.push(pushpin);
                <%}%>

            }
        </script>

    </head>
<body onload="getMap();">
     <div id='myMap' style="position:relative; width:1000px; height:400px;"></div>
     <div>
         <input type="button" value="AddPushpins" onclick="addPushpins();" />
     </div>
    </body>
</html>
```

The majority of this code listing will be familiar from Chapter 2, as the basic map remains the same. The main difference is the addition of the function addPushpins() and the button AddPushpins that calls it. In the function addPushpins, we use the default pushpin option and we specify the location of the pushpins by iterating through the list of Earthquake models and adding a pushpin for each one at item.Location.Latitude and item.Location.Longitude.

You will note the use of the <%= %> tags. These tags are to use the model in the aspx file. Thus, every time you refer to the model, you will surround the reference with the tags.

```
var pushpin = new Microsoft.Maps.Pushpin(new Microsoft.Maps.Location(
  <%=item.Location.Latitude%>, <%=item.Location.Longitude%>), pushpinOptions);
```

Additionally, we added a pushpin option that added the corresponding magnitude of each earthquake object as the text of the pushpin.

```
var pushpinOptions = { text: '<%=item.Magnitude%>', visible: true, textOffset: offset };
```

If you run this project, you will see a Bing map that displays the earthquake data that we retrieved in Chapters 3 and 4. (Note: your pushpins will be in different locations than ours, as your earthquake data will not be the same as ours.)

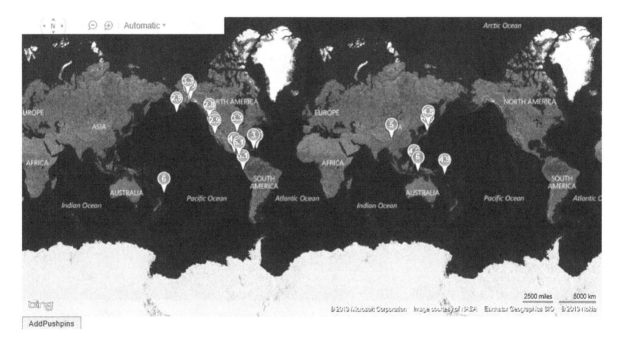

Figure 5-10. *Bing map displaying Earthquake data at their locations with their corresponding magnitudes*

Wrapping Up

Bing Maps Ajax Control allows you to create web-based Bing map applications with minimal effort. The online Interactive SDK creates the majority of the code snippets you will need, so much of the work required can be done by copy-paste! If you have a basic understanding of ASP.NET and MVC programming, a simple application such as the sample application in this chapter can be written in a couple of hours. In this chapter, we covered pushpins and polygons. In the subsequent chapter, we will be showing you how you can go even further with the APIs and build rich map applications using Bing Maps!

CHAPTER 6

▨ ▨ ▨

Doing More with Bing Maps

So you have now learned to build your first Bing Map web application. You can display geodata on a Bing map using pushpins. You even learned how to draw some basic geometric shapes. Now it's time for the fun stuff! Bing Maps can go so much further than the basic application we showed you in Chapter 5. Using Bing Maps REST (Representational State Transfer) Services, you'll be able to calculate routes between waypoints, or query for traffic incidences and much more. The Bing Maps REST Services API consist of the following APIs:

- **Location API**: Find a location based on an address or query
- **Elevations API**: Returns the elevation of a location, path or given Earth area
- **Imagery API**: Returns a static map or Bing Maps imagery information
- **Route API**: Calculates routes between two waypoints, or from a major road. You can also select either driving or walking directions.
- **Traffic API**: Used to get traffic information or other road incidences such as construction.

In addition to the REST services, Bing Maps AJAX Control v7 offers modules providing much of the same functionality as the REST services without needing to go through the REST services. For example, rather than querying the REST service for routes, you can also load the Bing.Maps.Directions module and request routes using that module instead. Some available modules are directions module, overlays module, and theme modules; however, you can also download custom modules or create your own.

In this chapter we will walk you through a few key services and other modules you can add for additional features and functionality. The functionalities we cover in this book are:

- **Location**: Determine a location based on an address or point of interest
- **Routing**: Determine the route between the given waypoints
- **Traffic**: Determine the current traffic conditions
- **Theming**: Applying the latest Bing Maps site designs in your own application

We will also show you how to create and add a custom module. There are, of course, other things you can do with Bing Maps; however, the APIs are similar enough to the ones we cover in this chapter that we refer you to the Bing Maps APIs online for the specifics.

Location

The first location-type question you might ask is "where is it?". For example, if we were to have the string "Beijing, China," we would like to be able to determine a latitude and longitude based on this query string. To answer this question, we use the Bing Maps REST Services and query for the location. Of course another location-type question we might ask is "where am I?". That question can be answered by the GeoLocationProvider class that is provided by the AJAX Control. We walk you through answering these two questions in the following sections.

Where is it?

The Location API gives you the ability to return the location in terms of latitude and longitude based on a query string. The REST call for such a query will appear as follows:

```
var searchRequest = 'http://dev.virtualearth.net/REST/v1/Locations/' + queryLocation +
'?output=json&jsonp=searchServiceCallback&key=' + 'Your Bing Map Key';
```

The query location string, *queryLocation*, can be something like "Seattle, WA". The Bing Map REST service will return either an XML or JSON response object. In this case, we have specified that a JSON object be returned, as we are working with Javascript code. Moreover, in the above query, we have specified the function callback to be searchServiceCallback.

Once you have the entire query search string, you pass this string, *searchRequest*, to the script, which appears as follows:

```
var mapscript = document.createElement('script');
mapscript.type = 'text/javascript';
mapscript.src = searchRequest;
document.getElementById('myMap').appendChild(mapscript)
```

You create a script document element, and set the type as Javascript, then you simply specify the source to be your query string. Let us walk you through a sample application that queries the Location REST API for locations and displays the results with pushpins on a map.

Sample Location Query Application

Once again we follow the standard MVC model from Chapter 5. Create a model named GeoLocation and paste code Listing 6-1 into it.

Listing 6-1. GeoLocation.cs. Model for a geo location

```
using System;
using System.Collections.Generic;
using System.Linq;
using System.Web;
using Microsoft.Maps.MapControl.WPF;

namespace MvcBingMapLocationByQuery.Models
{
    public class GeoLocation
    {
        public string LocationName { get; set; }
        public string City { get; set; }
        public Location Location { get; set; }

        public GeoLocation(string locationName, string city, Location where)
        {
            LocationName = locationName;
            City = city;
            Location = where;
        }
    }
}
```

Note, you should be adding the reference for *Microsoft.Maps.MapControl.WPF*. The model will be populated by the controller, which you create and name HomeController.cs and paste Listing 6-2 into it.

Listing 6-2. HomeController.cs. Controller populates the model class with geo location data and passes the data to the view

```
using System;
using System.Collections.Generic;
using System.Linq;
using System.Web;
using System.Web.Mvc;
using MvcBingMapLocationByQuery.Models;
using Microsoft.Maps.MapControl.WPF;

namespace MvcBingMapLocationByQuery.Controllers
{
    public class HomeController : Controller
    {
        //
        // GET: /Home/

        public ActionResult Index()
        {
            var locations = GetLocations();
            return View(locations);
        }

        public List<GeoLocation> GetLocations()
        {
            var locations = new List<GeoLocation>();
            var loc1 = new Location(37.788302, -122.408513);
            var geoLoc1 = new GeoLocation("Union Square", "San Francisco", loc1);
            var loc2 = new Location(37.436703, -122.160273);
            var geoLoc2 = new GeoLocation("Stanford University", "Palo Alto", loc2);
            locations.Add(geoLoc1);
            locations.Add(geoLoc2);

            return locations;
        }

    }
}
```

Finally, you right-click on the *Index( )* function declaration and you add a View, *Index.ascx*. As in Chapter 5, you will want to create a strongly typed view to the GeoLocation model. Once this is created, you can paste Listing 6-3.

Listing 6-3. Index. Ascx. Displays the map with the pushpins indicating the resulting locations of the query strings

```
<%@ Control Language="C#" Inherits="System.Web.Mvc.ViewUserControl<List<MvcBingMapLocationByQuery
.Models.GeoLocation>>" %>
```

```
<!DOCTYPE html PUBLIC "-//W3C//DTD XHTML 1.0 Transitional//EN"
"http://www.w3.org/TR/xhtml1/DTD/xhtml1-transitional.dtd">
<html>
    <head>
        <title>Find a location by query</title>
        <meta http-equiv="Content-Type" content="text/html; charset=utf-8"/>
        <script type="text/javascript"
src="http://ecn.dev.virtualearth.net/mapcontrol/mapcontrol.ashx?v=7.0"></script>
        <script type="text/javascript">
            var map = null;
            var query;
            function getMap() {
                map = new Microsoft.Maps.Map(document.getElementById('myMap'), { credentials: 'Your
Bing Map Key' });
            }

            function findLocation() {
                query = '<%=Model[0].City%>';
                map.getCredentials(callSearchService);
                query = '<%=Model[1].City%>';
                map.getCredentials(callSearchService);

            }

            function callSearchService(credentials) {
                var searchRequest = 'http://dev.virtualearth.net/REST/v1/Locations/' + query +
'?output=json&jsonp=searchServiceCallback&key=' + credentials;
                var mapscript = document.createElement('script');
                mapscript.type = 'text/javascript';
                mapscript.src = searchRequest;
                document.getElementById('myMap').appendChild(mapscript)
            }

            function searchServiceCallback(result) {
                var output = document.getElementById("output");
                if (output) {
                    while (output.hasChildNodes()) {
                        output.removeChild(output.lastChild);
                    }
                }
                var resultsHeader = document.createElement("h5");
                output.appendChild(resultsHeader);

                if (result &&
                result.resourceSets &&
                result.resourceSets.length > 0 &&
                result.resourceSets[0].resources &&
                result.resourceSets[0].resources.length > 0) {
                    resultsHeader.innerHTML = "Bing Maps REST Search API  <br/>  Found location " +
result.resourceSets[0].resources[0].name;
                    //var bbox = result.resourceSets[0].resources[0].bbox;
```

```
                   //var viewBoundaries = Microsoft.Maps.LocationRect.fromLocations(new Microsoft
.Maps.Location(bbox[0], bbox[1]), new Microsoft.Maps.Location(bbox[2], bbox[3]));
                   map.setView({ center: new Microsoft.Maps.Location(<%=Model[1].Location.
Latitude%>,<%=Model[1].Location.Longitude%>), zoom: 9 });
                   var location = new Microsoft.Maps.Location(result.resourceSets[0].resources[0].
point.coordinates[0], result.resourceSets[0].resources[0].point.coordinates[1]);
                   var pushpin = new Microsoft.Maps.Pushpin(location);
                   map.entities.push(pushpin);
               }
           else {
               if (typeof (response) == 'undefined' || response == null) {
                   alert("Invalid credentials or no response");
               }
               else {
                   if (typeof (response) != 'undefined' && response && result && result
.errorDetails) {
                       resultsHeader.innerHTML = "Message :" + response.errorDetails[0];
                   }
                   alert("No results for the query");

               }
           }
       }


    </script>
  </head>
  <body onload="getMap();">
    <div id='myMap' style="position:relative; width:1000px; height:500px;"></div>
    <div>
       <input type="button" value="FindLocation" onclick="findLocation();" />
    </div>
    <div id="output"></div>
  </body>
</html>
```

In the function findLocations, we get the query names of 'San Francisco' and 'Palo Alto' and then pass these names to the function callSearchService which performs the REST query. Finally the function searchServiceCallback sets the map view and adds a pushpin at the resulting locations returned from the Location REST query. Figure 6-1 shows the final output of this sample application.

Figure 6-1. *Location results for query of San Francisco and Palo Alto*

Where am I?

The GeoLocationProvider class will return the user's current location with compatible browsers, which support the W3C GeoLocation API (http://dev.w3.org/geo/api/spec-source.html). In Listing 6-2, we provide the code for requesting the user's location. The main difference between this code listing and previous View listings are the following commands:

```
var geoLocationProvider = new Microsoft.Maps.GeoLocationProvider(map);
geoLocationProvider.getCurrentPosition();
```

Listing 6-2. Returns the user's current location and displays it on a map

```
<%@ Control Language="C#" Inherits="System.Web.Mvc.ViewUserControl<dynamic>" %>

<!DOCTYPE html PUBLIC "-//W3C//DTD XHTML 1.0 Transitional//EN"
"http://www.w3.org/TR/xhtml1/DTD/xhtml1-transitional.dtd">
<html>
    <head>
        <title>Get location</title>
        <meta http-equiv="Content-Type" content="text/html; charset=utf-8"/>
        <script type="text/javascript" src="http://ecn.dev.virtualearth.net/mapcontrol/mapcontrol
.ashx?v=7.0"></script>
        <script type="text/javascript">
            var map = null;
```

```
        function getMap() {
            map = new Microsoft.Maps.Map(document.getElementById('myMap'), { credentials: 'Your
Bing Map Key' });
        }

        function getCurrentLocation() {
            var geoLocationProvider = new Microsoft.Maps.GeoLocationProvider(map);
            geoLocationProvider.getCurrentPosition();
            //alert('Current location set, based on your browser support for geo location API');
        }
    </script>
</head>
<body onload="getMap();">
    <div id='myMap' style="position:relative; width:1000px; height:500px;"></div>
    <div>
        <input type="button" value="GetCurrentLocation" onclick="getCurrentLocation();" />
    </div>
    <div id='output'> </div>
</body>
</html>
```

We instantiate the GeoLocationProvider class and initialize it with our map. Then we call getCurrentPosition to return the position. In Figure 6-2, we show you the resulting map, assuming the user was located on Stanford campus.

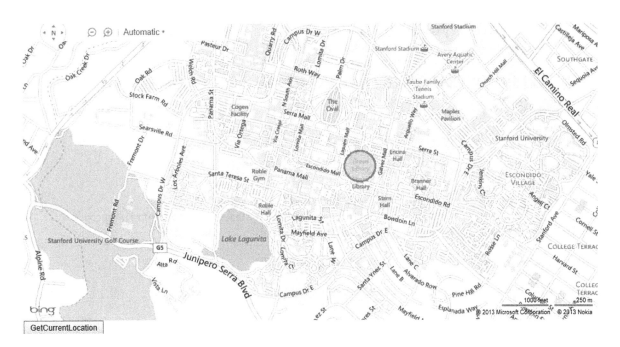

Figure 6-2. *User's geo location displayed on a Bing Map*

Routing

Perhaps one of the most common tasks for which people use maps is routing. Bing Maps provides a Routing REST API that returns routing instructions between waypoints. In this section we will show you how you can use this API to integrate this in your own map applications. The first thing you will need to familiarize yourself with is the Routing REST query string, which will appear as follows:

```
var routeRequest = 'http://dev.virtualearth.net/REST/v1/Routes?wp.0=' + start + '&wp.1=' + end +
'&routePathOutput=Points&output=json&jsonp=routeCallback&key=' + credentials;
```

You will note that the query string is quite similar to the query string for making a location query. The request is made to http://dev.virtualearth.net/REST/v1/Routes and is passed waypoints (wp). In this case, we have added two waypoints, start and end. Again we use a JSON response object. The query string is then passed to the javascript in the same fashion as with the location query:

```
var mapscript = document.createElement('script');
mapscript.type = 'text/javascript';
mapscript.src = routeRequest;
document.getElementById('myMap').appendChild(mapscript);
```

Sample Routing Query Application

The sample will use much of the same code as the Location Query sample application. The model will be the same GeoLocation.cs model from Listing 6-1, and the controller will be the same as Listing 6-2. The main difference will be in the View, which will now be pasted from Listing 6-4:

Listing 6-4. Index.ascx. View to display map with routing instructions

```
<%@ Page Language="C#" Inherits="System.Web.Mvc.ViewPage<List<MvcBingMapRouting.Models
.GeoLocation>>" %>

<!DOCTYPE html>

<html>
<head>
    <title>Find directions</title>
    <meta http-equiv="Content-Type" content="text/html; charset=utf-8" />
    <script type="text/javascript" src="http://ecn.dev.virtualearth.net/mapcontrol/mapcontrol.
ashx?v=7.0"></script>
    <script type="text/javascript">
        var map = null;
        var end;
        var start;

        function getMap() {
            map = new Microsoft.Maps.Map(document.getElementById('myMap'), { credentials: 'Your Bing
Map Key' });
        }
```

```
        function callRouteService(credentials) {
            var routeRequest = 'http://dev.virtualearth.net/REST/v1/Routes?wp.0=' + start +
'&wp.1=' + end + '&routePathOutput=Points&output=json&jsonp=routeCallback&key=' + credentials;
            var mapscript = document.createElement('script');
            mapscript.type = 'text/javascript';
            mapscript.src = routeRequest;
            document.getElementById('myMap').appendChild(mapscript);
        }

        function routeCallback(result) {
            var output = document.getElementById("output");
            if (output) {
                while (output.hasChildNodes()) {
                    output.removeChild(output.lastChild);
                }
                var resultsHeader = document.createElement("h5");
                var resultsList = document.createElement("ol");
                output.appendChild(resultsHeader);
                output.appendChild(resultsList);
            }

            if (result && result.resourceSets && result.resourceSets.length > 0 && result
.resourceSets[0].resources && result.resourceSets[0].resources.length > 0) {
                resultsHeader.innerHTML = "Bing Maps REST Route API  <br/>  Route from " + result
.resourceSets[0].resources[0].routeLegs[0].startLocation.name + " to " + result.resourceSets[0]
.resources[0].routeLegs[0].endLocation.name;
                var resultsListItem = null;

                for (var i = 0; i < result.resourceSets[0].resources[0].routeLegs[0].itineraryItems
.length; ++i) {
                    resultsListItem = document.createElement("li");
                    resultsList.appendChild(resultsListItem);
                    resultStr = result.resourceSets[0].resources[0].routeLegs[0].itineraryItems[i]
.instruction.text;
                    resultsListItem.innerHTML = resultStr;
                }
                var bbox = result.resourceSets[0].resources[0].bbox;
                var viewBoundaries = Microsoft.Maps.LocationRect.fromLocations(new Microsoft.Maps
.Location(bbox[0], bbox[1]), new Microsoft.Maps.Location(bbox[2], bbox[3]));
                map.setView({ bounds: viewBoundaries });
                var routeline = result.resourceSets[0].resources[0].routePath.line; var routepoints
= new Array();
                for (var i = 0; i < routeline.coordinates.length; i++) {
                    routepoints[i] = new Microsoft.Maps.Location(routeline.coordinates[i][0],
routeline.coordinates[i][1]);
                }
                var routeshape = new Microsoft.Maps.Polyline(routepoints, { strokeColor: new
Microsoft.Maps.Color(200, 0, 0, 200) });
```

```
            var startPushpinOptions = { anchor: new Microsoft.Maps.Point(10, 32) };
            var startPin = new Microsoft.Maps.Pushpin(new Microsoft.Maps.Location(routeline
.coordinates[0][0], routeline.coordinates[0][1]), startPushpinOptions);

            var endPushpinOptions = { anchor: new Microsoft.Maps.Point(10, 32) };
            var endPin = new Microsoft.Maps.Pushpin(new Microsoft.Maps.Location(routeline
.coordinates[routeline.coordinates.length - 1][0], routeline.coordinates[routeline.coordinates.length
- 1][1]), endPushpinOptions);
            map.entities.push(startPin);
            map.entities.push(endPin);
            map.entities.push(routeshape);
        }

        else {
            if (typeof (result.errorDetails) != 'undefined') {
                resultsHeader.innerHTML = result.errorDetails[0];
            }
            alert("No Route found");
        }
    }

    function getDirections() {
        start = '<%=Model[0].LocationName%>, ' + '<%=Model[0].City%>'; end = '<%=Model[1]
.LocationName%>, ' + '<%=Model[1].City%>';
            map.getCredentials(callRouteService);
        }

    </script>
</head>
<body onload="getMap();">
    <div id='myMap' style="position: relative; width: 1000px; height: 500px;"></div>
    <div>
        <input type="button" value="GetDirections" onclick="getDirections();" />
    </div>
    <div id="output"></div>

</body>
</html>
```

In this sample application, we pass the view two waypoints, Union Square in San Francisco and Stanford University in Palo Alto, along with their corresponding locations. The view parses these locations and requests routing instructions between the waypoints. In *routeCallback( )*, the map is then populated with pushpins from one waypoint to the other, and a *polyline* shape is drawn to reflect the routing directions by connecting the points along the routeline. You will recall that we covered how to draw polylines in Chapter 5, and now you know why! The result of this sample application will look like Figure 6-3.

GetDirections

Bing Maps REST Route API
Route from Union Square, CA to Stanford University, CA

1. Depart Post St toward Stockton St
2. Turn right onto Stockton St
3. Turn left onto 4th St
4. Take ramp right and follow signs for I-80 West
5. Keep straight onto US-101 S
6. At exit 408, take ramp right for CA-84 West toward Seaport Blvd
7. Bear right onto CA-84 W / Woodside Rd
8. Take ramp right toward El Camino Real South
9. Turn right onto Redwood Ave, and then immediately turn right onto CA-82 S / El Camino Real
10. Turn right onto Galvez St
11. Arrive at Stanford University, CA

Figure 6-3. Routing directions between Union Square, San Francisco and Stanford University, Palo Alto

Alternatively, rather than using the REST Services, you can load the Directions module.

Directions Module

Using the Direction module, you can also get routing information. In Listing 6-5, we show you how to get driving directions using the module. In order to use this module, you must first load the module. In the function `createDirections`, you will find the command to load the directions module:

```
Microsoft.Maps.loadModule('Microsoft.Maps.Directions', { callback: createDrivingRoute })
```

This command then calls the function that will create waypoints and set them to the start and end points of the route. You may, of course, have additional waypoints along the way. This example uses the same start and end points as the previous example. You will note that you can set a waypoint to either an address or to a specific latitude and longitude.

Listing 6-5. Creating Driving directions using the Directions module

```
<%@ Page Language="C#" Inherits="System.Web.Mvc.ViewPage<List<MvcBingMapsDirections.Models
.GeoLocation>>" %>

<!DOCTYPE html PUBLIC "-//W3C//DTD XHTML 1.0 Transitional//EN"
"http://www.w3.org/TR/xhtml1/DTD/xhtml1-transitional.dtd">
<html>
    <head>
        <title>Create Driving Route</title>
        <meta http-equiv="Content-Type" content="text/html; charset=utf-8"/>
        <script type="text/javascript" src="http://ecn.dev.virtualearth.net/mapcontrol/mapcontrol
.ashx?v=7.0"></script>
        <script type="text/javascript">
            var map = null;
            var directionsManager;
            var directionsErrorEventObj;
            var directionsUpdatedEventObj;

            function getMap() {
                map = new Microsoft.Maps.Map(document.getElementById('myMap'), { credentials: 'Your
Bing Map Key' });
            }

            function createDirectionsManager() {

                if (!directionsManager)
                {
                    directionsManager = new Microsoft.Maps.Directions.DirectionsManager(map);
                }


                directionsManager.resetDirections();
                directionsErrorEventObj = Microsoft.Maps.Events.addHandler(directionsManager,
'directionsError' );
                directionsUpdatedEventObj = Microsoft.Maps.Events.addHandler(directionsManager,
'directionsUpdated');
            }

            function createDrivingRoute() {
                if (!directionsManager) { createDirectionsManager(); }
                directionsManager.resetDirections();
                // Set Route Mode to driving
                directionsManager.setRequestOptions({ routeMode: Microsoft.Maps.Directions.RouteMode
.driving });
                var Waypoint1 = new Microsoft.Maps.Directions.Waypoint({ address: '<%=Model[0].
LocationName%>, <%=Model[0].City%>' });
                directionsManager.addWaypoint(Waypoint1);
                var Waypoint2 = new Microsoft.Maps.Directions.Waypoint({ location: new Microsoft.Maps
.Location(<%=Model[1].Location.Latitude%>, <%=Model[1].Location.Longitude%>) });
                directionsManager.addWaypoint(Waypoint2);
```

```
                // Set the element in which the itinerary will be rendered
                directionsManager.setRenderOptions({ itineraryContainer:
document.getElementById('directionsItinerary') });
                directionsManager.calculateDirections();
            }

        function createDirections() {
            if (!directionsManager) {
                Microsoft.Maps.loadModule('Microsoft.Maps.Directions', { callback:
createDrivingRoute });
            }
            else {
                createDrivingRoute();
            }
        }
        </script>
    </head>
 <body onload="getMap();">
    <div id='myMap' style="position:relative; width:1000px; height:500px;"></div>
    <div>
        <input type="button" value="CreateDrivingRoute" onclick="createDirections();" />
    </div>
    <div id='directionsItinerary'> </div>
  </body>
</html>
```

In Figure 6-4, we show you the resulting map and directions.

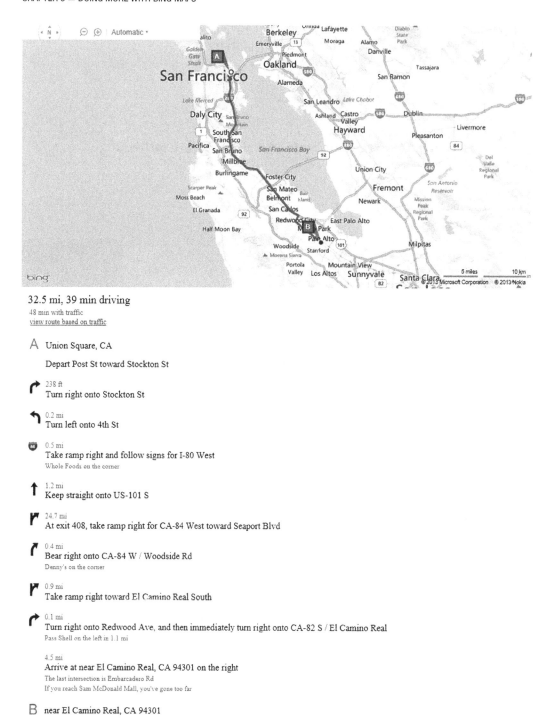

32.5 mi, 39 min driving

48 min with traffic
view route based on traffic

A Union Square, CA

Depart Post St toward Stockton St

↱ 238 ft
Turn right onto Stockton St

↰ 0.2 mi
Turn left onto 4th St

⬤ 0.5 mi
Take ramp right and follow signs for I-80 West
Whole Foods on the corner

↑ 1.2 mi
Keep straight onto US-101 S

↱ 24.7 mi
At exit 408, take ramp right for CA-84 West toward Seaport Blvd

↱ 0.4 mi
Bear right onto CA-84 W / Woodside Rd
Denny's on the corner

↱ 0.9 mi
Take ramp right toward El Camino Real South

↱ 0.1 mi
Turn right onto Redwood Ave, and then immediately turn right onto CA-82 S / El Camino Real
Pass Shell on the left in 1.1 mi

4.5 mi
Arrive at near El Camino Real, CA 94301 on the right
The last intersection is Embarcadero Rd
If you reach Sam McDonald Mall, you've gone too far

B near El Camino Real, CA 94301

Figure 6-4. *Driving directions using the Directions Module*

Rather than driving directions, you may want to get walking or transit directions instead. With the Directions module, you are also able to do so quite easily. Simply change the route mode from driving to either walking or transit as follows:

```
directionsManager.setRequestOptions({ routeMode: Microsoft.Maps.Directions.RouteMode.walking });

directionsManager.setRequestOptions({ routeMode: Microsoft.Maps.Directions.RouteMode.transit });
```

Traffic

If directions are one of the key map use cases, then checking traffic information is right up there with it. Thankfully, Bing Maps also provides a REST Service that allows for quick and easy querying of traffic information. Like with routing, the Bing Maps AJAX Control v7 also provides a traffic module. If what you want is just to view the current traffic conditions, you can load a traffic module for the map as follows:

```
var trafficLayer = new Microsoft.Maps.Traffic.TrafficLayer(map);
trafficLayer.show();
```

You will want to set the view of the map to center on the particular area of interest, using *map.setView()*. In Listing 6-6, we show you the full listing of displaying traffic conditions of a given location that we pass to the View from the model.

Listing 6-6. Displaying traffic conditions on a map for a given location

```
<%@ Page Language="C#" Inherits="System.Web.Mvc.ViewPage<List<MvcBingMapTraffic.Models
.GeoLocation>>" %>

<!DOCTYPE html>

<html>
    <head>
        <title>Add/Show Traffic Layer</title>
        <meta http-equiv="Content-Type" content="text/html; charset=utf-8"/>
        <script type="text/javascript" src="http://ecn.dev.virtualearth.net/mapcontrol/mapcontrol
.ashx?v=7.0"></script>
        <script type="text/javascript">
            var map = null;
            function trafficModuleLoaded() {
                setMapView();
            }
            function loadTrafficModule() {
                Microsoft.Maps.loadModule('Microsoft.Maps.Traffic', { callback: trafficModuleLoaded });
            }
            function setMapView() {
                map.setView({ zoom: 10, center: new Microsoft.Maps.Location(<%=Model[0].Location
.Latitude%>,<%=Model[0].Location.Longitude%>) })
            }
            function getMap() {
                map = new Microsoft.Maps.Map(document.getElementById('myMap'),
{ credentials: 'At_LKBdN_d_G9Y6N53J-GtmMY8ZB-1iEc8hMlwoq6tlNldu-nkGkDPMnaye_a6XT' });
                loadTrafficModule();
            }
            function showTrafficLayer() {
```

```
                    var trafficLayer = new Microsoft.Maps.Traffic.TrafficLayer(map);
                    // show the traffic Layer
                    trafficLayer.show();
                }
            </script>
        </head>
    <body onload="getMap();">
            <div id='myMap' style="position:relative; width:1000px; height:500px;"></div>
            <div>
                <input type="button" value="ShowTrafficLayer" onclick="showTrafficLayer();" />
            </div>
            <div id='output'> </div>
        </body>
</html>
```

In Figure 6-5 we show you the traffic conditions around Union Square, San Francisco.

Figure 6-5. *Traffic conditions for a given location*

Sometimes you will want to get specific traffic incidences. For example, you may want to determine if there was a road accident or there is some construction. The Traffic REST API allows you to query for this information. A basic query will look like the following:

The REST query to retrieve traffic information is as follows:

```
var trafficRequest = 'http://dev.virtualearth.net/REST/v1/Incidents/' + latitude1 + ',' + longitude1
+ ',' + latitude2 + ',' + longitude2 + '?key=' + credentials;
```

In the above query we have specified a bounding box for which we want the traffic incidences returned. Aside from the MapArea, there are a number of other optional fields that can be included in the query:

- **includeLocationCodes**: a boolean parameter that defaults to false. It returns the location codes, which provide pre-defined road segment traffic information.

- **Severity**: Indicates the severity of the incident. The return value is from 1 (Low Impact) to 4 (Serious)

- **Type**: Specifies the type of traffic incident to return. There are 11 different types:

1. Accident

2. Congestion

3. DisabledVehicle

4. MassTransit

5. Miscellaneous

6. OtherNews

7. PlannedEvent

8. RoadHazard

9. Construction

10. Alert

11. Weather

A sample JSON response could be as follows:

```
{
    "authenticationResultCode":"ValidCredentials",
    "brandLogoUri":"http:\/\/dev.virtualearth.net\/Branding\/logo_powered_by.png",
    "copyright":"Copyright © 2011 Microsoft and its suppliers. All rights reserved. This API cannot
be accessed and the content and any results may not be used, reproduced or transmitted in any manner
without express written permission from Microsoft Corporation.",
    "resourceSets":[
        {
            "estimatedTotal":131,
            "resources":[
                {
"__type":"TrafficIncident:http:\/\/schemas.microsoft.com\/search\/local\/ws\/rest\/v1",
                    "point":{
                        "type":"Point",
                        "coordinates":[
                            38.85135,
                            -94.34033
                        ]
                    },
                    "congestion":"",
                    "description":"MO-150 is closed between 5th Ave S and Court Dr - construction",
                    "detour":"",
                    "end":"\/Date(1310396400000)\/",
                    "incidentId":210546697,
```

```
                "lane":"",
                "lastModified":"\/Date(1309391096593)\/",
                "roadClosed":true,
                "severity":3,
                "start":"\/Date(1307365200000)\/",
                "type":9,
                "verified":true
            },
            {
"__type":"TrafficIncident:http:\/\/schemas.microsoft.com\/search\/local\/ws\/rest\/v1",
                "point":{
                    "type":"Point",
                    "coordinates":[
                        38.85872,
                        -94.54638
                    ]
                },
                "congestion":"",
                "description":"Botts Rd is closed between Andrews Rd and 142nd St - construction",
                "detour":"To go north take US-71 NB to 140th St and go west on 140th St to access
Botts Rd- To go south continue west on MO-150 to Thunderbird Rd to 149th St",
                "end":"\/Date(1315244760000)\/",
                "incidentId":191097424,
                "lane":"",
                "lastModified":"\/Date(1309391096593)\/",
                "roadClosed":true,
                "severity":1,
                "start":"\/Date(1295704800000)\/",
                "type":9,
                "verified":true
            }
        ]
    }
    ],
    "statusCode":200,
    "statusDescription":"OK",
    "traceId":"38491198bf6a42f5b7e60c18aa08ec02"
}
```

Alternatively, by specifying the output parameter to be (o=xml), you can receive an XML output instead.

Theming

You may want to apply the latest Bing Maps site designs to your own applications. For this, you will use the Theme module. As with the other modules, you will load the theme module using the *loadModule*( ) command. We already showed you how you could add pushpins in Chapter 5, but alternatively, you can add pushpins using the theme module. In Listing 6-7, we show you how you can add a pushpin and infobox for a given location. The below code places a pushpin in the given location and adds an information box containing the name of the point of interest. Again, we have used the same model and controller as all the other sample applications in this chapter, so you will not be surprised by the pushpins located at Union Square and Stanford University shown in Figure 6-6. Upon mousing over one of the pushpins, the infobox appears.

Listing 6-7. Theme module to add pushpins and infoboxes.

```
<%@ Control Language="C#" Inherits="System.Web.Mvc.ViewUserControl<List<MvcBingMapTheming.Models.
GeoLocation>>" %>

<!DOCTYPE html PUBLIC "-//W3C//DTD XHTML 1.0 Transitional//EN"
"http://www.w3.org/TR/xhtml1/DTD/xhtml1-transitional.dtd">
<html>
                <head>
                <title>Load map with navigation bar module</title>
                <meta http-equiv="Content-Type" content="text/html; charset=utf-8"/>
                <script type="text/javascript" src="http://ecn.dev.virtualearth.net/mapcontrol/
mapcontrol.ashx?v=7.0"></script>
                <script type="text/javascript">
                    var map = null;
                    function getMap() {
                        Microsoft.Maps.loadModule('Microsoft.Maps.Themes.BingTheme', {
                            callback: function () {
                                map = new Microsoft.Maps.Map(document.getElementById('myMap'),
                        {
                            credentials: 'Your Bing Maps Key,
                            theme: new Microsoft.Maps.Themes.BingTheme()
                        });
                                var pin1 = new Microsoft.Maps.Pushpin(new Microsoft.Maps
.Location(<%=Model[0].Location.Latitude%>,<%=Model[0].Location.Longitude%>), null);
                                map.entities.push(pin1);
                                map.entities.push(new Microsoft.Maps.Infobox(new Microsoft.Maps
.Location(<%=Model[0].Location.Latitude%>,<%=Model[0].Location.Longitude%>), { title: '<%=Model[0]
.LocationName%>', description: 'description here', pushpin: pin1 }));
                                var pin2 = new Microsoft.Maps.Pushpin(new Microsoft.Maps.
Location(<%=Model[1].Location.Latitude%>,<%=Model[1].Location.Longitude%>), null);
                                map.entities.push(pin2);
                                map.entities.push(new Microsoft.Maps.Infobox(new Microsoft.Maps.
Location(<%=Model[1].Location.Latitude%>,<%=Model[1].Location.Longitude%>), { title: '<%=Model[1].
LocationName%>', description: 'description here', pushpin: pin2 }));
                                map.setView({ center: new Microsoft.Maps.Location(<%=Model[0].
Location.Latitude%>,<%=Model[0].Location.Longitude%>), zoom: 10});
                            }
                        });
                    }
                </script>
                </head>
                <body onload="getMap();">
                <div id='myMap' style="position:relative; width:1000px; height:500px;"></div>
                </body>
</html>
```

Figure 6-6. Pushpin and Infobox added using the Theme module

Building Your Own Modules

Up until now, we have shown you how to use the out-of-the-box modules that Bing Maps AJAX control has provided for you. One of the nice features is that you can build your own module and include those in your web application.

The first thing you will want to do is to build the module itself. In Listing 6-8, we have written a simple javascript module that takes four locations and draws a polygon using those locations as the vertices.

Listing 6-8. Self-made module that draws a polygon for given locations

```
// polygonmodule.js

function PolygonModule(map)
{
   // Draw a polygon using the given locations as vertices
   this.drawPolygon = function(location0, location1, location2, location3)
      {
         // Initialize the polygon locations
         var points = new Array(5);
         points[0] = location0;
         points[1] = location1;
         points[2] = location2;
         points[3] = location3;
         points[4] = location0;
         var polyline = new Microsoft.Maps.Polyline(points, null);
```

```
        map.entities.push(polyline);

    }
}
Microsoft.Maps.moduleLoaded('PolygonModule');
```

This module has a function *drawPolygon* that draws the actual polygon. The last line in the module is the *Microsoft.Maps.moduleLoaded('PolygonModule')*, which is essential for calling the main code's callback function. This module must now be hosted on a web server of your choosing.

Next, you must register the module:

```
Microsoft.Maps.registerModule("PolygonModule", "http://YourWebServer/polygonmodule.js");
```

And then you can load the module much in the same way you've loaded the pre-built modules:

```
Microsoft.Maps.loadModule("PolygonModule", { callback: myModuleLoaded });
```

Finally, you can call the module. We use Union Square in San Francisco as our locations, much in the same way we did in Chapter 5, when you learned how to draw a polygon. Unsurprisingly, the resulting map looks the same as it did in Chapter 5, despite the use of a drawing polygon module, as you can observe in Figure 6-7. This example is somewhat silly as it is abstracting a function that requires no abstraction, but we kept it simple so the code listing would be easy to follow. The full code listing for the view is in Code Listing 6-9.

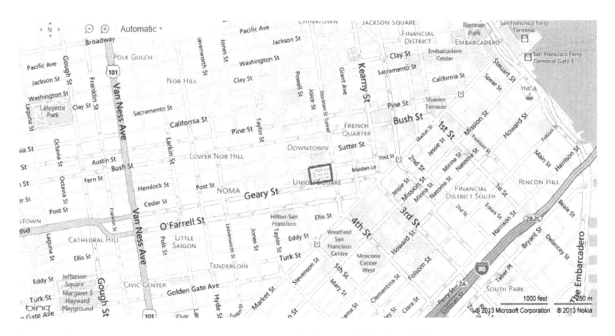

Figure 6-7. *Polygon drawn around Union Square using the Polygon Module in Code Listing 6-8*

Listing 6-9. Calling the custom module

```
<%@ Page Language="C#" Inherits="System.Web.Mvc.ViewPage<List<MvcBingMapsModules.Models.GeoLocation>>" %>

<!DOCTYPE html PUBLIC "-//W3C//DTD XHTML 1.0 Transitional//EN"
"http://www.w3.org/TR/xhtml1/DTD/xhtml1-transitional.dtd">
<html>
    <head>
        <title></title>
        <meta http-equiv="Content-Type" content="text/html; charset=utf-8">

        <script type="text/javascript"
src="http://ecn.dev.virtualearth.net/mapcontrol/mapcontrol.ashx?v=7.0"></script>

        <script type="text/javascript">

            var map;

            function myModuleLoaded() {
                var polygonModule = new PolygonModule(map);
                polygonModule.drawPolygon(new Microsoft.Maps.Location(37.788327, -122.408447),
                    new Microsoft.Maps.Location(37.788531, -122.406837),
                    new Microsoft.Maps.Location(37.787607, -122.406676),
                    new Microsoft.Maps.Location(37.787412, -122.408264));

                map.setView({zoom: 15, center: new Microsoft.Maps.Location(<%=Model[0].Location
.Latitude%>,<%=Model[0].Location.Longitude%>) })
            }

            function GetMap() {
                // Initialize the map
                var options = { credentials: "Your Bing Map Key" };
                map = new Microsoft.Maps.Map(document.getElementById('mapDiv'), options);

                // Register and load the arrow module
                Microsoft.Maps.registerModule("PolygonModule", "http://YourWebServer/polygonmodule.js");
                Microsoft.Maps.loadModule("PolygonModule", { callback: myModuleLoaded });

            }

        </script>
    </head>
    <body onload="GetMap();">
        <div id='mapDiv' style="position:relative; width:1000px; height:500px;"></div>
    </body>
</html>
```

Wrapping Up

In this chapter, you learned how to do more with Bing Maps for web-based applications. Routing, geolocating, and querying for traffic information have all become basic use cases for maps. We showed you how to do that using either the REST Services or the AJAX Control modules. The beauty of the modules is Bing Maps allows you to build your own modules. In subsequent chapters you will learn how to create Bing map applications for other platforms such as Windows Phone.

CHAPTER 7

Bing Maps for WPF

Web applications are well and good, but not every application is well suited to being a web application. Sometimes, what's called for is a plain, old-fashioned, double-clickable executable, either because of business or feature constraints. Location-enabling a .NET application isn't any more difficult than adding a Bing Maps assembly and control. In this chapter and the next, we show you how to do this first for Windows Presentation Foundation (WPF) and then for the Windows Store for Windows 8.

In this chapter, we show you the ins and outs of using Bing Maps in WPF applications. As you might imagine from Microsoft, it's as easy as adding an assembly to your project and writing a bit of XAML and code-behind to get started. You'll learn what the control is capable of, how to configure a project to include the control, and the basic organization of classes in the control. Then we dive into coding with the control, showing you first a simple "Hello Map" application, followed by the WPF version of our Earthquake application, and wrap up with examples of how to use the two Bing Maps services that are part of Bing Maps but not the control: the geocoding and routing services.

Introducing the Bing Maps for WPF Control

The features and design of the Bing Maps for WPF control will be pretty familiar to you if you studied our description of the Web control, but there are some differences. Like the AJAX control for the web, the WPF control:

- Provides a rendering of the world in aerial, street, and hybrid (aerial plus roads) modes using raster tiles.

- Supports free panning and zooming using traditional affordances (mouse, touch, scrollwheel, and pinch-to-zoom).

- Permits you to add layers that contain polygons, polylines, and map markers.

There are key differences, however. Most notably, you construct your user interface around the map and its components using the Extensible Application Markup Language (XAML) you already know and love as a Windows developer. As you see later in the chapter, you can even construct map markers in XAML. On the feature side, it largely has parity with the AJAX control, although as we write this, there's no support for traffic display.

Note Like the AJAX control, the Bing Maps for WPF control requires a connection to the Internet to obtain its map tiles. You can use the control in your WPF application even if the computer running your application is not connected to the Internet, but it will not be able to download or render maps without an Internet connection!

Getting the Control

The Bing Maps for WPF control is made available as an assembly from the Microsoft Download Center: go to http://bit.ly/16xHcy1 or do a Bing search for "Bing Maps WPF Control", download the installer, and follow the installation instructions. It requires the .NET Framework 4.0 and the Windows SDK, both of which you should have installed if you have a recent version of Microsoft Visual Studio installed.

Just as with the AJAX control, you'll need a Bing Maps key; if you skipped getting one when you read Chapter 2, now's your chance. Follow the steps there, registering for a Windows Live ID if you don't have one and then getting a Bing Maps Basic API Key. You can prototype your application without one, but you'll get a big nasty message every time you display a map about how you need an API key, so it's easier just to get one and get it over with, especially before you show your application to anyone else.

Once you get the control SDK installed, you'll need to add a reference to its assembly in your WPF application. Doing this is the same as adding any other assembly:

1. Select the solution you'd like to add the reference to,

2. Right-click and choose "Add Reference. . .",

3. In the dialog that appears, click "Browse" on the left, and then press the "Browse. . ." button,

4. Navigate to the directory where the Bing Maps for WPF Control assembly is (by default, you should find it in C:\Program Files (x86)\Bing Maps WPF Control\V1\Libraries).

Key Classes and Relationships

The Bing Maps for WPF assembly has four namespaces you need to use in your application:

- The Microsoft.Maps.MapControl.WPF namespace, which contains the workhorse classes you're likely to use the most when you use the control, like Map and MapLayer.

- The Microsoft.Maps.MapControl.WPF.Core namespace has fundamental classes like exceptions and enumerations used in the implementation of the control.

- The Microsoft.Maps.MapControl.WPF.Design namespace is ill-named in our opinion, because it doesn't have anything to do with design per se, and instead contains classes for parsing and data type conversion.

- The Microsoft.Maps.MapControl.WPF.Overlays namespace contains the implementation of default overlays you may want to place on a map, like the compass overlay or the scale control that shows the map scale.

When you use the control, you'll usually start by instantiating one or more instances of Map (in Microsoft.Maps.MapControl.WPF), configuring it and wiring some event handlers to it, and possibly configuring one or more overlays with data to overlay on the map.

Two key properties you need to be aware of that the Map control has are the CredentialProvider and the Mode properties You specify your API key as the value of the CredentialProvider attribute; failing to do this lets the map control load, but not without a note across the front saying you need to include the API key. The Mode attribute lets you pick what kind of data the map control displays. Choices include:

- Road: Shows the street network in a symbolic mode.

- Aerial: Shows an aerial view from the nadir perspective.

- AerialWithLabels: Shows an aerial view from the nadir perspective and includes road labels as you zoom in.

Map inherits from `MapCore`, which is where you'll find most of the methods you expect for a map control, including:

- The `Center` property which you can set or get to determine the map's geographic center. The value of this property is an instance of the Location lass, which bears the latitude and longitude of the location.

- The `ZoomLevel` property which you can set or get to determine the current zoom level of the map. Higher values indicate more zoom; a `ZoomLevel` of 1 shows the whole world, while approximately 10 shows city-level detail, and approximately 20 is the highest level of detail you can presently render.

The `MapCore` class also has the very handy `TryLocationToViewportPoint` and `TryViewportPointToLocation` methods, which you use when you need to convert between a latitude and longitude and the corresponding view point on the map. It also has a number of `SetView` methods, which let you center the map on a point with a specific zoom level, or indicate that a specific geographic rectangle should be shown (at which point the control determines the appropriate center coordinate and zoom level to ensure that the rectangle you specify is in view).

Events generated by the `Map` control are split between the `MapCore` and `Map` classes; as you might imagine, the usual bevy of user events for things like key, touch, and mouse events. There are some specific events you may want to watch for, however:

- The `ModeChanged` event, which occurs when the map mode (aerial, road, or both) changes.

- The `ViewChangeStart` and `ViewChangeEnd` events, which occur at the beginning and end of animated transitions, respectively. (There's also a `ViewChangeOnFrame` event, if you want to synchronize something to animation frame display.)

As those events suggest, the map control includes animation when transitioning from one position to another. Generally, that's something you want: animation between the current viewpoint and a new viewpoint gives the user something to look at while the data loads, and provides some orientation to the user as well. The `Map` class has a property, `AnimationLevel`, which can be set to one of the following `AnimationLevel` values:

- `Full`, indicating that animation should happen both when properties are mutated and as a result of user input,

- `None`, indicating that no animation should occur, or

- `UserInput`, indicating that animation should occur only as a result of user input.

Bing Maps gives you a few custom layers called *overlays*; these overlays let you show and hide:

- the map compass, indicating which way is north (the `Compass` class)

- the copyright information for the map (the `Copyright` class)

- the Bing logo (the `Logo` class),

- and the map scale (using the `Scale` class).

Like the AJAX version of the control, you organize additional information for the map control to display in layers. The assembly provides the `MapLayer` class, a class that positions its child elements using geographic, rather than viewpoint, coordinates. `MapLayer` instances are glorified `Panel` instances; most of the class's interface relates to child management, or the bookkeeping necessary to map between map geocoordinates and view coordinates. Odds are you'll make one or more `MapLayer` instances and add child objects to it, and then show or hide those layers to make your map data visible or invisible.

Map Pushpins let you mark individual points on the map. They have a `Location` property, which lets you specify the location of a pushpin on the map in geocoordinates, as well as a heading, indicating how the pushpin should be rotated. They're full citizens of the WPF world, meaning that they can generate all the events an interactive control can (touch, stylus, mouse, and keyboard), and can have a `Template` property that indicates what the pushpin should look like (the default is an orange circle with a stem). You can also plot lines and polygons on the map using the `MapPolyline` and `MapPolygon` classes; these use `Location` instances for their points.

Using the Control

Enough generalities—let's dig in and write some code using the Bing Maps control. We begin with a simple example to show you how to display a map and process events from the map, and then move on from there to our sample application, and close our discussion with an example that ties together the Bing Maps control with the Bing Maps services for geocoding and routing.

Kicking the Tires

Let's begin with a "Hello Map" style application. Open Visual Studio and:

1. Create a new C# WPF application. We called ours "WPFHelloMap".

2. Add a reference to the Bing Maps for WPF assembly. Right-click the project, choose "Add Reference", and navigate to Microsoft.Maps.MapControl.WPF.dll.

3. Add a namespace for the Bing Maps assembly and your Bing Maps API key as a resource to your App.xaml file. It should look something like this:

```
<Application x:Class="WPFHelloMap.App"
  xmlns="http://schemas.microsoft.com/winfx/2006/xaml/presentation"
  xmlns:x="http://schemas.microsoft.com/winfx/2006/xaml"
  xmlns:map="clr-namespace:Microsoft.Maps.MapControl.WPF;
assembly=Microsoft.Maps.MapControl.WPF"
  StartupUri="MainWindow.xaml">
  <Application.Resources>
    <map:ApplicationIdCredentialsProvider
      x:Key="MyCredentials"
      ApplicationId="your-id" />
  </Application.Resources>
</Application>
```

4. Open the MainWindow.xaml file, add a namespace for the assembly, and add an instance of the Map class. While you're at it, you might want to make the window a little bigger:

```
<Window x:Class="WPFHelloMap.MainWindow"
  xmlns="http://schemas.microsoft.com/winfx/2006/xaml/presentation"
  xmlns:x="http://schemas.microsoft.com/winfx/2006/xaml"
  xmlns:map="clr-namespace:Microsoft.Maps.MapControl.WPF;
assembly=Microsoft.Maps.MapControl.WPF"
  Title="MainWindow" Height="600" Width="800">
  <Grid>
    <map:Map
      x:Name="Map"
      Mode="AerialWithLabels"
      HorizontalAlignment="Stretch"
      VerticalAlignment="Stretch"
      AnimationLevel="Full"
      CredentialsProvider="{StaticResource MyCredentials}" >
    </map:Map>
  </Grid>
</Window>
```

5. Run the application. You should be rewarded with a window containing an aerial map of the world, as you see in Figure 7-1. Try panning and zooming the map with your mouse (or finger, if you're running Windows 8 on a touch-enabled device).

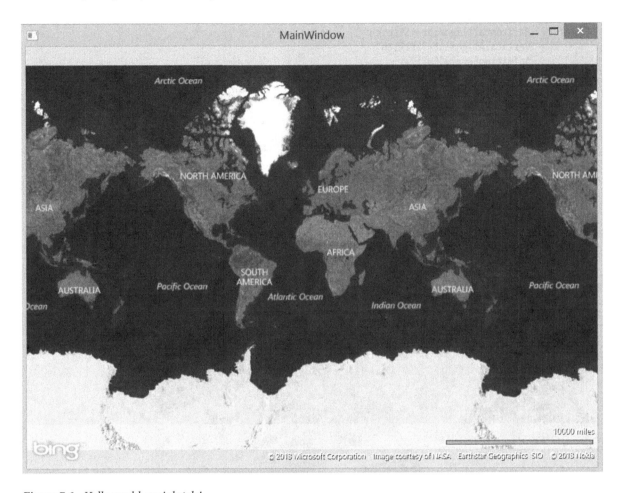

Figure 7-1. *Hello world, aerial style!*

This is just basic XAML; let's do a bit more XAML hacking and add a button that centers the map on one of our favorite coffee shops.

1. Add a button someplace to the XAML and wire up a click handler for it. You can just slap down a button over the map with the code here, or do something fancier with a Grid layout (which we did, as you can see from the next figure).

```
<Button Height="32" Width="128" Content="Show Red Rock" Click="Button_Clicked"/>
```

2. Add some XAML for a pushpin inside the `map:Map` tag:

```
<map:Map
  x:Name="Map"
  Mode="AerialWithLabels"
  HorizontalAlignment="Stretch"
  VerticalAlignment="Stretch"
  AnimationLevel="Full"
    CredentialsProvider="{StaticResource MyCredentials}" >
    <map:Pushpin
      Location="37.39366,-122.07888"/>
</map:Map>
```

3. Add the following to the code-behind in MainWindow.xaml.cs. Make sure you include the `using` directive at the top of the code-behind:

```
using Microsoft.Maps.MapControl.WPF;
...
public void Button_Clicked(object sender, RoutedEventArgs e)
{
    Location redrock = new Location(37.39366,-122.07888);
    Map.SetView(redrock, 20);
}
```

4. Run the app and push the button. You'll see a short animation to Red Rock in Mountain View (Figure 7-2).

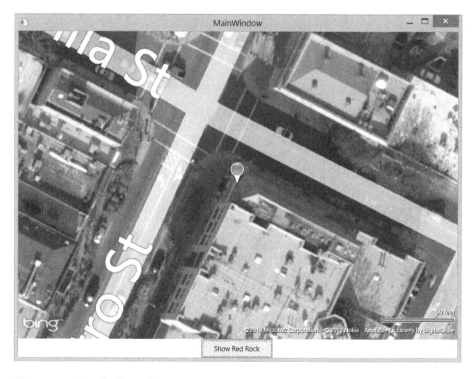

Figure 7-2. *A push pin on the map*

Finally, let's hook up an event handler to the map: we'll add an event handler to the map that shows your latitude and longitude wherever you click.

1. Add the event bindings to your XAML:

```
<map:Map Grid.Row="0"
  x:Name="Map"
  Mode="AerialWithLabels"
  HorizontalAlignment="Stretch"
  VerticalAlignment="Stretch"
  AnimationLevel="Full"
  MouseUp="Map_MouseUp"
  CredentialsProvider="{StaticResource MyCredentials}" >
```

2. Add the code-behind for the event to show a message box:

```
private void Map_MouseUp(object sender, MouseButtonEventArgs e)
{
    Location ll = Map.ViewportPointToLocation(e.GetPosition(Map));
    MessageBox.Show(ll.Latitude + "," + ll.Longitude);
}
```

Try it out and see (Figure 7-3)!

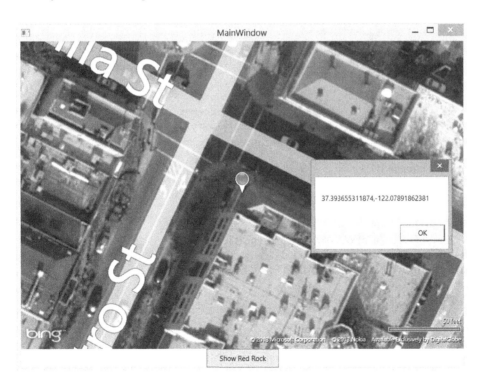

Figure 7-3. *Click handling*

Earthquakes Everywhere!

Let's take a look at a more involved sample, our earthquake application, which you can see in Figure 7-4. Most of the interesting code is in the XAML, so let's look at that first, in Listing 7-1.

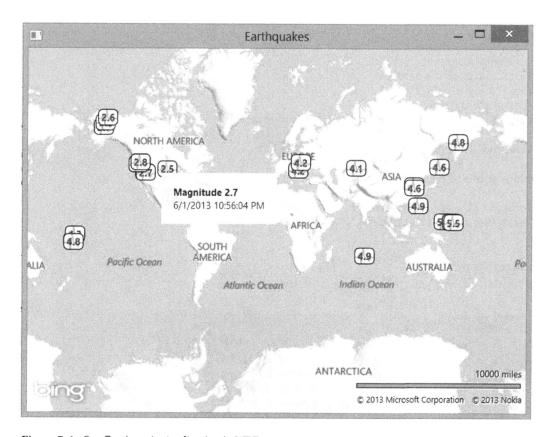

Figure 7-4. *Our Earthquake Application in WPF*

Listing 7-1. The MainWindow.xaml for the Earthquake application

```
<Window x:Class="WPFMapApplication.MainWindow"
  xmlns="http://schemas.microsoft.com/winfx/2006/xaml/presentation"
  xmlns:x="http://schemas.microsoft.com/winfx/2006/xaml"
  xmlns:map="clr-namespace:Microsoft.Maps.MapControl.WPF;
assembly=Microsoft.Maps.MapControl.WPF"
  Title="Earthquakes" Height="480" Width="640">

<Window.Resources>
  <BitmapImage x:Key="EarthquakeIcon" UriSource="Resources/icon.png" />
  <ControlTemplate x:Key="CustomPushpinTemplate" TargetType="map:Pushpin">
    <Grid x:Name="ContentGrid"
          HorizontalAlignment="Center"
          VerticalAlignment="Center">
```

```xml
    <StackPanel>
        <Grid Margin="0" Width="25" Height="20">
         <Rectangle Fill="White"
            Stroke="#FF000000"
            RadiusX="5" RadiusY="5"/>
          <Image Source="Resources/icon.png"
            Width="25" Height="20" Opacity="0.25" />
            <ContentPresenter HorizontalAlignment="Center"
              VerticalAlignment="Center"
              Content="{TemplateBinding Content}"
              ContentTemplate="{TemplateBinding ContentTemplate}"
              Margin="0"
              TextBlock.FontFamily="Segoe UI"
              TextBlock.FontWeight="Bold"
              TextBlock.Foreground="#FFB8000B"/>
        </Grid>
      </StackPanel>
    </Grid>
  </ControlTemplate>

  <DataTemplate x:Key="EarthquakeTemplate">
    <map:Pushpin map:MapLayer.Position="{Binding Location}"
     Tag="{Binding}"
     MouseEnter="Pushpin_MouseEnter"
     MouseLeave="Pushpin_MouseLeave"
     Template="{StaticResource CustomPushpinTemplate}"
     Content="{Binding Magnitude}"/>
  </DataTemplate>
</Window.Resources>

<Grid>
  <map:Map x:Name="DisplayMap"
    CredentialsProvider="{StaticResource MyCredentials}">
    <map:Map.Children>
      <map:MapItemsControl
        ItemsSource="{Binding Earthquakes}"
        ItemTemplate="{StaticResource EarthquakeTemplate}"/>

      <map:MapLayer x:Name="ContentPopupLayer">
        <Grid x:Name="ContentPopup"
          Visibility="Collapsed"
          Background="White"
          Opacity="0.85">
          <StackPanel Margin="15">
            <TextBlock x:Name="ContentPopupText"
              FontSize="12"
              FontWeight="Bold"/>
            <TextBlock x:Name="ContentPopupDescription"
              FontSize="12"/>
          </StackPanel>
        </Grid>
```

```
        </map:MapLayer>
      </map:Map.Children>
    </map:Map>
  </Grid>
</Window>
```

First up is a `ControlTemplate` for the custom pushpin we use to mark the location of each earthquake.

Next up is a `DataTemplate`, which encapsulates the pushpin itself. It maps the `Content` of the pushpin to the earthquake's magnitude (we'll show you the model and `Earthquake` class later) and assigns a couple of event handlers so we can show more detail about the earthquake when you hover over the pushpin.

The map itself in the `Grid` view is straightforward, but this is the first time we've shown you a `MapItemControl`. It's a class that lets you use a `MapLayer` as an `ItemsPanel`—essential if you want to bind data to an `ItemSource` and `ItemTemplate`, which is what we do here. The template is our `DataTemplate` containing our custom `Pushpin`, and the data behind the binding will be our list of earthquakes.

Finally, we use a custom `MapLayer` to wrap a `StackPanel` that will show the earthquake's magnitude and date/timestamp when you hover over a pushpin. We use a `MapLayer` here, rather than a conventional layer, because we want to position the text legend in geographic space, rather than the pixel space of the control (so that the legend hovers near the earthquake event with a minimum of coding on our part to achieve this).

The code-behind for the XAML is straightforward (we've eliminated the `using` directives and the namespace for brevity); it's in Listing 7-2.

Listing 7-2. The code-behind for Earthquake's user interface

```
public partial class MainWindow : Window
{
  public MainWindow()
  {
    InitializeComponent();
    DataContext = new EarthquakeViewModel();
  }

  private void Pushpin_MouseEnter(object sender, MouseEventArgs e)
  {
    FrameworkElement pin = sender as FrameworkElement;
    MapLayer.SetPosition(ContentPopup, MapLayer.GetPosition(pin));
    MapLayer.SetPositionOffset(ContentPopup, new Point(20, -20));

    var quake = (Earthquake)pin.Tag;

    ContentPopupText.Text = "Magnitude " + quake.Magnitude;
    ContentPopupDescription.Text = quake.When.ToString();
    ContentPopup.Visibility = Visibility.Visible;
  }

  private void Pushpin_MouseLeave(object sender, MouseEventArgs e)
  {
    ContentPopup.Visibility = Visibility.Collapsed;
  }
}
```

Our constructor needs to configure the `DataContext` with our data model.

The MouseEnter handler for the pushpin must figure out where to position the context popup that will contain the earthquake information details; it does this by getting the position of the pin generating the event and setting the ContentPopup's position to that pin, offset by a small amount. It then reads the data associated with that pin (an Earthquake object) and populates the context popup with the data before setting the popup's visibility to show the popup. The MouseLeave handler just flips the visibility, hiding the popup.

The Earthquake class (Listing 7-3) is a straight-up data container class, and needs no further explanation.

Listing 7-3. The Earthquake class

```
public class Earthquake
{
  public string Title { get; set; }
  public string Description { get; set; }
  public double Magnitude { get; set; }
  public Location Location { get; set; }
  public DateTime When { get; set; }
  public Earthquake(Location where,
                    DateTime when,
                    double magnitude,
                    string title,
                    string description = "")
  {
    Location = where;
    When = when;
    Magnitude = magnitude;
    Title = title;
    Description = description;
  }
}
```

The model is equally simple (Listing 7-4).

Listing 7-4. The EarthquakeViewModel class

```
public class EarthquakeViewModel : INotifyPropertyChanged
{
  private ObservableCollection<Earthquake> _earthquakes;
  public ObservableCollection<Earthquake> Earthquakes
  {
    get { return _earthquakes; }
    set
    {
      _earthquakes = value;
      OnPropertyChanged("Earthquakes");
    }
  }

  public EarthquakeViewModel()
  {
    USGSEarthquakeService.GetRecentEarthquakes((o, ea) =>
    {
      Earthquakes = new ObservableCollection<Earthquake>(ea.Locations);
    });
  }
```

```
  public event PropertyChangedEventHandler PropertyChanged;
  protected virtual void OnPropertyChanged(string propertyName)
  {
    if (PropertyChanged != null)
      PropertyChanged(this, new PropertyChangedEventArgs(propertyName));
  }
}
```

The only interesting thing going on here is in the constructor, where we populate the model from our USGS Earthquake service, which is backed by the WCF service you saw us write in Chapter 4.

Geocoding with the Bing Maps Geocoder Service

Although not formally part of the Bing Maps control, the Bing Maps Geocoder service lets you determine the latitude and longitude of an address, or map the nearest address to a given latitude and longitude. It's a prerequisite for things like routing, in which your users are likely thinking in terms of addresses and the service is thinking in terms of geocoordinates. Using the Bing Maps Geocoder Service is just like using any other SOAP service. You need to add a service reference to the Geocoding service at http://dev.virtualearth.net/webservices/v1/geocodeservice/geocodeservice.svc. The resulting interface, IGeocodeService, has four methods:

- Geocode, which takes an address request and determines its geolocation,

- GeocodeAsync, an asynchronous version of Geocode,

- ReverseGeocode, which takes a position and determines its approximate address,

- and ReverseGeocodeAsync, an asynchronous version of ReverseGeocode.

These take a GeocodeRequest, which has fields for things like the address and position of a location. Listing 7-5 shows how to perform a simple geocoding request.

Listing 7-5. Geocoding an address

```
BingGeocodeService.GeocodeResult result = null;

using (BingGeocodeService.GeocodeServiceClient client =
  new BingGeocodeService.GeocodeServiceClient("CustomBinding_IGeocodeService"))
{
  BingGeocodeService.GeocodeRequest request =
    new BingGeocodeService.GeocodeRequest();
  request.Credentials = new Credentials()
  {
    ApplicationId = (App.Current.Resources["MyCredentials"] as
      ApplicationIdCredentialsProvider).ApplicationId
  };
  request.Query = address;
  result = client.Geocode(request).Results[0];
}
return result;
```

The only thing here you should take careful note of is that you must provide your Bing API key as the request `Credentials`. The result structure includes the following fields:

- `Address` contains the address of the resulting reverse geocode, if one was found, or the original address for a geocoding operation.

- `Locations` contains the latitude and longitude of the location.

- `Confidence` indicates the geocoder's confidence in the result.

We'll use the geocoder in the next section, when we route between two locations.

Routing with the Bing Maps Routing Service

Our last example for the chapter shows how to compute a route with the Bing Maps Routing Service, another SOAP service hosted by Microsoft. As you see in Figure 7-5, it plots a route from downtown Sunnyvale to the café that so occupied our maps at the beginning of the chapter, Red Rock Coffee.

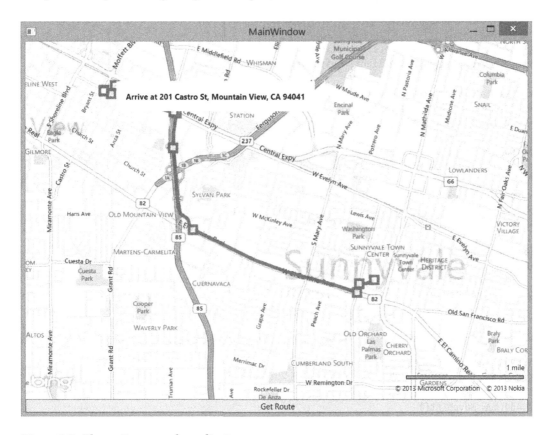

Figure 7-5. *The routing example application*

To use the Bing Maps Routing Service, you'll need to add the service endpoint to your application. It's at `http://dev.virtualearth.net/webservices/v1/routeservice/routeservice.svc`.

Our routing is done in our view model, which geocodes the source and destination positions, calculates a route, and then converts the route to a MapPolyline we show on the map. Listing 7-6 shows the relevant parts of the view model.

Listing 7-6. Determining a route and populating the data model's Waypoints field

```
private ObservableCollection<Waypoint> _waypoints;
public ObservableCollection<Waypoint> Waypoints
{
  get { return _waypoints; }
  set
  {
    _waypoints = value;
    OnPropertyChanged("Waypoints");
  }
}
private void CalculateRoute(BingGeocodeService.GeocodeResult from,
  BingGeocodeService.GeocodeResult to)
{
  using (BingRouteService.RouteServiceClient client =
    new BingRouteService.RouteServiceClient("CustomBinding_IRouteService"))
  {
    BingRouteService.RouteRequest request =
      new BingRouteService.RouteRequest();
    request.Credentials = new Credentials()
    {
      ApplicationId = (App.Current.Resources["MyCredentials"] as
        ApplicationIdCredentialsProvider).ApplicationId
    };
    request.Waypoints = new BingRouteService.Waypoint[2];
    request.Waypoints[0] = ConvertGeocodeResultToWaypoint(from);
    request.Waypoints[1] = ConvertGeocodeResultToWaypoint(to);

    request.Options = new BingRouteService.RouteOptions();
    request.Options.RoutePathType = BingRouteService.RoutePathType.Points;

    RouteResult = client.CalculateRoute(request).Result;
  }

  Waypoints = new ObservableCollection<Waypoint>();

  foreach (BingRouteService.ItineraryItem item
    in RouteResult.Legs[0].Itinerary)
  {
    Waypoints.Add(new Waypoint()
      {
        Description = GetDirectionText(item),
        Location = new Location(item.Location.Latitude,
          item.Location.Longitude)
      });
  }
}
```

The Route Service takes an array of waypoints along a route (so multi-stop routing is possible) and options such as whether the route should be for cars or pedestrians, and returns a list of ItineraryItem objects, one for each leg of the route. The ItineraryItem class has a lot of fields about a decision point along a route, including:

- The compass direction at the decision point to take.

- The location of the decision point (which we use here as the vertexes of our geographic polyline).

- The description of the maneuver at the decision point.

- Warnings about the maneuver.

In this example, we just stash aside the location of the decision point and the text for the maneuver in a container class, which we use to populate our polyline. The XAML uses the data from the model to show turn-by-turn directions at each decision point; when the model changes, we update the route line on the map by throwing away the old route line and creating a new one (Listing 7-7).

Listing 7-7. Creating a MapPolyline from the route

```
private static void OnRouteResultChanged(Map map,
  BingRouteService.RouteResult oldValue,
  BingRouteService.RouteResult newValue)
{
  MapPolyline line = new MapPolyline();
  line.Locations = new LocationCollection();
  line.Opacity = 0.80;
  line.Stroke = new SolidColorBrush(Colors.Magenta);
  line.StrokeThickness = 5.0;

  foreach (BingRouteService.Location l in newValue.RoutePath.Points)
  {
    line.Locations.Add(new Location(l.Latitude, l.Longitude));
  }

  var layer = GetRouteLineLayer(map);
  if (layer == null)
  {
    layer = new MapLayer();
    SetRouteLineLayer(map, layer);
  }

  layer.Children.Clear();
  layer.Children.Add(routeLine);

  LocationRect rect = new LocationRect(
    routeLine.Locations[0],
    routeLine.Locations[routeLine.Locations.Count - 1]);
  map.SetView(rect);
}
```

This code just creates a new polyline from the points along the route, and adds it as the sole child of a `MapLayer` to contain the route line. (As you can see from this and the prior code, a lot of the code you need to write when working with the Bing Map SOAP services is just interconversion code to get from the service-layer classes to the appropriate Bing Maps classes, and vice versa.)

The XAML just ties together the model, the map, and the layers for the polyline and the decision point text box.

Wrapping Up

In this chapter, we've walked you through the basics of getting the Bing Maps for WPF control integrated with your WPF application as well as how to use it along with the Bing Maps SOAP services in a C# application.

The control itself is a full participant in WPF, handling map tile fetching, rendering, and generating app-level events for user and map actions such as touch, mouse, and keyboard. As with other WPF controls, you can express most of your user interface in XAML, saving C# code for the code-behind that handles events and provides a data model to the map to indicate what to display.

Microsoft also provides two SOAP services available to your application with your API key, one for geocoding and one for routing. You can use these as part of your location-aware applications, either in conjunction with map display or as separate components that add location-aware features for your own purposes.

CHAPTER 8

Bing Maps for Windows Store Apps

Like it or not, Windows 8 is Microsoft's answer to the growing market for tablets, providing a new user interface that spans mouse and touch, running on both Intel and ARM processors. A flagship feature of Windows 8 is the Windows Store, and the applications you can purchase from it. Windows Store applications—previously called Metro or Modern applications—sport a new, touch-friendly user interface that's suited to a wide variety of devices. If you're planning to target Windows with a commercial application, targeting Windows Store should be a very high priority in your plan.

In this chapter, we show you the support that Bing Maps brings to Windows Store applications. If you have read the previous chapters on the various Bing Maps control interfaces, there's a lot here that should be familiar to you. However, there are some new capabilities that are different from the Bing Maps for WPF control that you'll want to take advantage of, and we go over them here. We also walk you through two sample applications that use the Windows Store version of the Bing Maps control, giving you plenty of experience with code you can use in your own applications.

Introducing Bing Maps for Windows Store

If you've read any of the previous chapters on the various Bing Map controls for different platforms, you're already starting to get the idea. For Windows Store apps, the Bing Maps control supports viewing maps in symbolic or aerial mode, with support for adding your own layers, pushpins, and shapes (filled and hollow). In addition, the version for Windows Store also includes:

- A new mode called bird's-eye mode that shows a combination of aerial footage and symbolic detail.

- The ability to turn on and off a traffic layer in many parts of the world, showing up-to-the-minute traffic on major roads.

- Support for clickable landmarks in many parts of the world, with underlying information about the landmark.

- Support for venue maps in the United States and some other countries, giving you additional map details about venues such as airports and shopping malls and their contents.

The Bing Maps for Windows Store application is available as a downloadable SDK. The SDK contains classes in two namespaces: `Bing.Maps` and `Bing.Maps.VenueMaps` described at `http://bit.ly/19rFL23`. Most of the classes you usually interact with are in the `Bing.Maps` namespace, although you may want to use the various classes representing specific venues that you find in the `Bing.Maps.VenueMaps` namespace. The organization of the `Bing.Maps` namespace is similar to the namespace for the Bing Maps WPF control and closely mirrors the interfaces you get when you use the Bing Maps AJAX control as well. It contains classes that represent a map, layers on a map, pushpins, and map shapes, as well as landmarks on a map. As you might imagine, there's a host of supporting classes too, for things like events.

At the heart of the Bing.Maps namespace is the Map class, which represents a map control on the screen. It's a subclass of Control, and has the usual properties you'd expect, including:

- Center, a Location that indicates the center of the map.

- Culture, the culture code of the map to use for localization.

- Credentials, which must contain your Bing Maps API key when you instantiate the control.

- Heading, the directional heading of the map in geometric degrees (0° corresponding to true north, 90° being east, and so forth).

- MapType, one of MapType.Aerial, MapType.Birdseye, MapType.Road, or MapType.Empty, indicating the map's type.

- MinZoomLevel and MaxZoomLevel, indicating the minimum and maximum amount that a map can be zoomed.

- MetersPerPixel, indicating the current scale in meters per pixel at the center of the map.

- RotationEnabled, indicating whether or not the map can be rotated by setting its Heading property.

- VenueManager, an instance of the Bing.Maps.Venue.VenueManager class for searching and displaying venues.

- ZoomLevel, the current map zoom level.

In addition, there are various bits that can be overlaid on the map; these are not layers in the sense of being MapLayer instances you manipulate, but rather additional Boolean properties that you can set or clear. These include:

- ShowBuildings, indicating whether or not the control shows building footprints on the map.

- ShowNavigationBar, which indicates whether or not the control shows map navigation controls (such as the map type selector).

- ShowBreadcrumb, which indicates whether or not the control shows a semantic hierarchy of the map's position across the top of the map (such as World > United States > MA > Suffolk Co. > Chelsea).

- ShowScaleBar, which indicates whether or not the control shows the scale bar.

- ShowTraffic, which indicates whether or not traffic is overlaid on the map.

The map control supports animated transitions, so you'll probably want to set the various properties through the public methods that are available. Chief among these is SetView, with overrides to recenter the map on a specific Location, recenter the map on a location at a possibly different zoom level, recenter the map on a location at a zoom level with a specific heading, and only show a specific georectangle. There's also SetZoomLevel, which lets you specify a new zoom level and optionally indicate how long the animation should take when shifting to the new zoom level. To handle coordinate transformations from geographic space to screen space, there are the TryLocationToPixel and TryPixelToLocation methods, which map to and from a geolocation on the map to its pixel position in screen coordinates.

The map generates a number of custom events that have to do with its underlying functionality, including events indicating when the map style changes, the target view changes, all of the map tiles have downloaded, and events for each frame of an animation and when an animation completes. Of course, internally it uses most of the UIElement classes for its own purposes, so when you want to catch events generated by the map control, you'll use the corresponding event that's named with the ending Override. For example, to catch an unhandled tap on the map, you use the TappedOverride event (and not the Tapped event, as you might guess). There are user interface events for taps, double taps, key down and up events, pointer movement, and scroll wheel movement.

To encapsulate a hierarchy of objects on the map, the SDK provides the MapLayer class, which lets you position objects on the map in geographic space. You can either create instances of MapLayer and work with them directly—often in XAML—or you can use the MapLayer class's static method SetPosition, which positions another object on the map, and then add the object directly to the map's Children property.

An obvious thing you can add to the map are Pushpin instances; these are small round circles that can have a text label, and are just about the right size for touching with a simple numeric label and nothing else. You can also add polygons or polylines with instances of the MapPolygon and MapPolyline classes; or you can add any XAML control you like. For example, to plop an image on a map control named map, you might write:

```
Image image = new Image();
image.Source = new BitmapImage(new Uri(BaseUri,"image.png"));
image.Width = 32;
image.Height = 32;
MapLayer.SetPosition(image, new Location(42.3713, -71.0642));
map.Children.Add(image);
```

The Bing Maps control for Windows Store apps has some additional semantic understanding of the world, encapsulated in its Landmark and Venue classes. In many parts of the world, points of interest on the map are clickable, and when you click them, the map control issues a LandmarkTapped event, including a Landmark with additional details about the landmark you tapped. Equally interesting is the addition of *venue maps* (Figure 8-1), which appear when you tap a venue such as an airport or shopping mall in many parts of the world. Venues are searchable, and you can gain additional information about the businesses in a venue, including their name, location, and phone number.

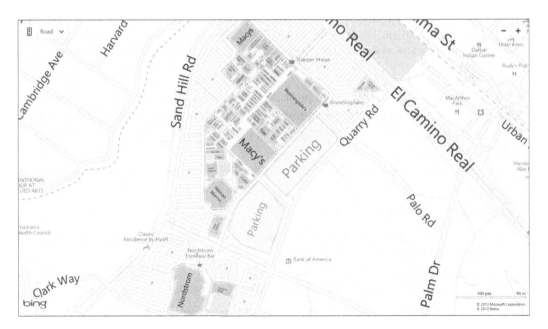

Figure 8-1. *A venue map in the Bing Maps control for Windows Store apps*

Interacting with venues is the responsibility of the VenueManager class. The Map class has an instance available through its VenueManager property; with it, you can:

- Determine the active venue on a map by checking the ActiveVenue property,

- Show or hide the control that lets the user pick a floor with the ShowFloorControl property,

119

- Set whether a venue outline displays when the mouse moves over a venue with the UseDefaultVenueOutline property,

- Control whether or not a tool tip displays when the mouse moves into the venue or clicks on a venue with the UseDefaultVenueTooltip property.

Not all countries have venue maps; you can obtain a list of which do by invoking the VenueManager's GetAllCountriesAsync method. You can search for venues near a point using the GetNearbyVenuesAsync method, too. Finally, the VenueManager manages its own pointer and tap events, so if you want to track user behavior while a venue map is active, you'll need to monitor the manager's events such as VenueTapped, which triggers when the user taps the venue itself.

A final class you'll likely want to know about is the MapItemsControl class, which represents a control to manage data binding. As with other data-binding controls, it has ItemsTemplate and ItemsSource properties to specify the binding relationship; you can bind the control to static lists or dynamic models, as we show you later in this chapter in our Earthquake example.

Seeing the Bing.Maps Map Control in Action

In the sections that follow, we show you how to start using the control, handle events from the control, examine venues and landmarks, and then wrap up with a look at the Earthquake sample we've been presenting throughout the book. It's worth noting that if you read the previous chapter on the control for WPF, you'll see many similarities. In fact, the Earthquake application is largely untouched; the key difference between the WPF and the Windows Store versions of the application have to do with how we construct the custom pushpin for the map.

Before you begin, be sure that you've registered for a Bing Maps API key (as we show you how to do in Chapter 2) and head over to http://bit.ly/19CJgle to download the Bing Maps SDK for Windows Store. Once you do that, you can add a reference to the Bing Maps SDK assembly to any application you're writing, and you should be all set.

■ **Note** The Bing Maps SDK assembly comes in versions specifically targeted to the various processors Windows supports. When building and running applications that use the SDK, avoid using the "Any CPU" option and instead choose a specific CPU target for your package, one of "ARM", "x86", or "x64". If you're writing C++ instead of C#, your choices are "ARM", "Win32", or "x64".

Your First Windows Store Map App

Beginning at the beginning, Listing 8-1 shows the XAML for a simple Windows 8 application that displays a map control in a Windows 8 page. We created this by:

1. Creating an empty Windows Store application in C# in Visual Studio
   (File ➤ New Project... ➤ Visual C# ➤ Windows Store ➤ Blank App (XAML))

2. Right-click the project and choose "Add Reference..." and add a reference to the Bing.Maps assembly by expanding "Windows" and selecting "Bing Maps" from the "Extensions" list item.

3. Putting the code you see in Listing 8-1 into the MainPage.xaml file, replacing the text "your-api-key" with your Bing Maps API key.

Listing 8-1. The simplest Windows Store map-enabled application

```
<Page
    x:Class="ModernAppMapSample.MainPage"
    xmlns="http://schemas.microsoft.com/winfx/2006/xaml/presentation"
    xmlns:x="http://schemas.microsoft.com/winfx/2006/xaml"
    xmlns:local="using:ModernAppMapSample"
    xmlns:d="http://schemas.microsoft.com/expression/blend/2008"
    xmlns:mc="http://schemas.openxmlformats.org/markup-compatibility/2006"
    xmlns:map="using:Bing.Maps"
    mc:Ignorable="d">

    <Grid Background="{StaticResource ApplicationPageBackgroundThemeBrush}">
            <map:Map Grid.Column="1" x:Name="map"
                    Credentials="your-api-key"/>
    </Grid>
</Page>
```

There's two things to pay attention to in this XAML: the namespace declaration for xmlns:map in the Page declaration, and the map:Map control instance in the grid.

This application code is enough to give you the basic map and venue map navigation most applications start out with; it was this application that we used to capture the screen shot back in Figure 1-1, and of course Figure 8-1.

Interacting with Landmarks and Venues

Let's look a little at the landmark and venue support this version of the map control brings. Change the XAML for your map control to read as you see in Listing 8-2.

Listing 8-2. Adding a bread crumb to the UI and an event handler to catch when landmarks are tapped

```
<map:Map Grid.Column="1" x:Name="map"
  Credentials="your-api-key"
  TappedOverride="Map_Tapped"
  LandmarkTapped="Map_LandmarkTapped"
  ShowBreadcrumb="True"/>
```

Now, edit your code-behind so that you have a Map_LandmarkedTapped method. In addition, add an event handler for when venues are tapped, as you see in Listing 8-3. Don't forget to either fully qualify the Bing Maps classes, or add using directives for both Bing.Maps and Bing.Maps.VenueMaps at the top of your file.

Listing 8-3. Event handlers for tapping the map, a landmark, and a venue.

```
public MainPage()
{
  this.InitializeComponent();
  VenueManager m = map.VenueManager;
  m.UseDefaultVenueTooltip = false;
  m.VenueEntityTapped += Venue_Tapped;
}
```

```
private void Venue_Tapped(object sender, VenueEntityEventArgs e)
{
  int i;
}

private void Map_Tapped(object sender, TappedRoutedEventArgs e)
{
  int i;
}

private void Map_LandmarkTapped(object sender, LandmarkTappedEventArgs e)
{
  int i;
}
```

The code in the constructor just adds an event handler to the VenueManager, of course; it's a little easier to do it that way than it is to do it in the XAML in this case the way you did with the TappedOverride and LandmarkTapped events.

Now, put breakpoints in each of your event handlers and re-run the application. You should see the breadcrumb bar at the top of the map control (Figure 8-2). You should zoom into an area in the United States and try tapping on landmarks and venues; you'll be able to enter the venue map mode, and then click on individual venues.

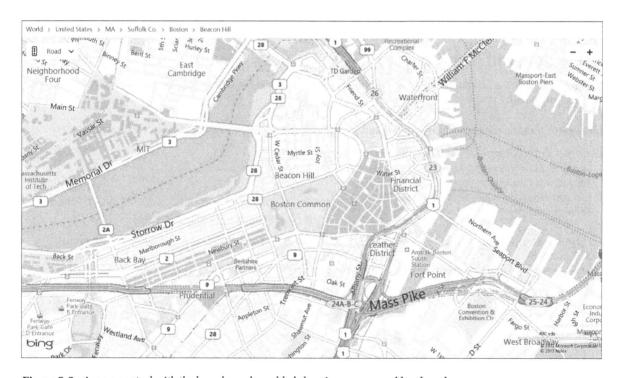

Figure 8-2. *A map control with the breadcrumb enabled showing venues and landmarks*

On the map, venues are a slightly more purple color than water; the easiest way to figure out what one looks like is go to an area with a venue and look at it, such as the venue to the east of Boston Common in Figure 8-2). The first tap on the venue activates the venue, loading the venue map into the control; subsequent taps generate VenueTapped events, which should trigger your breakpoint.

Landmarks are the little labeled spots on a map, like the entrances to Fenway Park you see in the southwest of Figure 8-2.

Creating a Custom Pushpin

Putting a conventional pushpin on the map is easy: you can do it in XAML with code such as:

```
<map:Map ...>
  <map:Map.Children>
    <map:Pushpin>
      <map:MapLayer.Position>
        <map:Location Latitude="42.3551" Longitude="-70.0659" />
      </map:MapLayer.Position>
    </map:Pushpin>
  </map:Map.Children>
</map:Map>
```

Let's create a custom pushpin that shows the latitude and longitude you've tapped. We did this with a combination of XAML hacking and a bit of fooling around in Blend; the results are in Listing 8-4. You can recreate this by adding a new user control to your sample project, and using the XAML, or experiment with Blend and make your own.

Listing 8-4. A custom pushpin to show the latitude and longitude

```
<UserControl
    x:Class="ModernAppMapSample.CustomPin"
    xmlns="http://schemas.microsoft.com/winfx/2006/xaml/presentation"
    xmlns:x="http://schemas.microsoft.com/winfx/2006/xaml"
    xmlns:local="using:ModernAppMapSample"
    xmlns:d="http://schemas.microsoft.com/expression/blend/2008"
    xmlns:mc="http://schemas.openxmlformats.org/markup-compatibility/2006"
    mc:Ignorable="d"
    d:DesignWidth="64" Height="64" Width="64">

  <Grid Margin="-32,-32,0,0" Width="64" Height="64">
    <Ellipse Fill="#FF1D1DF5"
      HorizontalAlignment="Left"
      Height="64"
      Stroke="Black"
      VerticalAlignment="Top"
      Width="64"
      Margin="-32,-32,0,0"/>
    <GridView HorizontalAlignment="Left"
      VerticalAlignment="Top"
      Height="64"
      Width="64"
      Margin="-32,-32,0,0"/>
    <TextBlock x:Name="latitude"
      HorizontalAlignment="Left"
      VerticalAlignment="Top"
      Margin="-20,-15,0,0"
      TextWrapping="Wrap"
      Text=""/>
```

```
    <TextBlock
      x:Name="longitude"
      HorizontalAlignment="Left"
      VerticalAlignment="Top"
      Margin="-20,5,0,0"
      TextWrapping="Wrap"
      Text=""/>
  </Grid>
</UserControl>
```

The XAML for our pushpin is pretty straightforward, although you may be wondering about the funky margins. When you add controls as pushpins to a map layer, they're positioned by the upper-right corner. For something like this, where we want to mark the center of a tap, we need to offset the control by half the size of the control, so that the upper corner is really at the center of the control.

Our custom control needs a bit of code-behind, too, so that it has latitude and longitude properties our event handlers can set. Listing 8-5 shows the code-behind for our control.

Listing 8-5. The code-behind for our custom pushpin

```
public sealed partial class CustomPin : UserControl
{
  public string Latitude {
    get { return latitude.Text; }
    set { latitude.Text = value; }
  }

  public string Longitude {
    get { return longitude.Text; }
    set { longitude.Text = value; }
  }

  public CustomPin()
  {
    this.InitializeComponent();
  }
}
```

Now, all that remains is to wire up the various event handlers we stubbed in back in Listing 8-3 to create and show an instance of our control. Listing 8-6 shows the result, and Figure 8-3 shows what happens when you click around the map.

Listing 8-6. Adding our custom pushpin to the map control

```
CustomPin m_pushPin;
private void Venue_Tapped(object sender, VenueEntityEventArgs e)
{
  if (e.VenueEntity != null)
  {
    Location location = e.VenueEntity.Location;
    ShowLatLong(location);
  }
}
```

```csharp
private void Map_Tapped(object sender, TappedRoutedEventArgs e)
{
  var position = e.GetPosition(map);
  Location location;
  map.TryPixelToLocation(position, out location);
  ShowLatLong(location);
}

private void Map_LandmarkTapped(object sender, LandmarkTappedEventArgs e)
{
  if (e.Landmarks.Count != 0)
  {
    ShowLatLong(e.Landmarks[0].Location);
  }
}

private void ShowLatLong(Location location)
{
  if (m_pushPin == null)
  {
    m_pushPin = new CustomPin();
    map.Children.Add(m_pushPin);
  }

  m_pushPin.Latitude =
    Math.Round(location.Latitude, 4).ToString();
  m_pushPin.Longitude =
    Math.Round(location.Longitude, 4).ToString();

  MapLayer.SetPosition(m_pushPin, location);
  map.SetView(location);
}
```

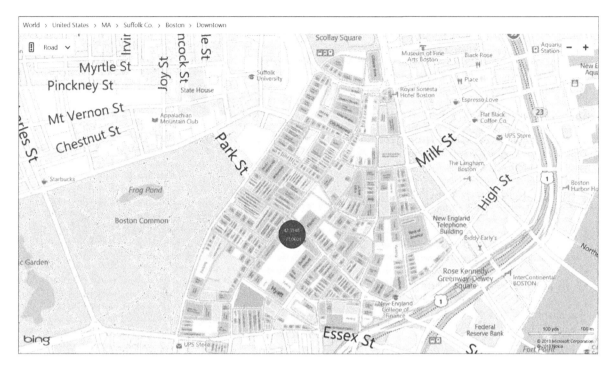

Figure 8-3. *Our custom pushpin on the map*

Listing 8-6 shows several bits of code that use the map control:

- The Venue_Tapped and Landmark_Tapped event handlers both examine the contents of the event to determine the geolocation of the thing that the user touched.

- The Map_Tapped event handler uses TryPixelToLocation to get the latitude and longitude that the user tapped.

- We lazily create a single map marker at the first time it's needed, and then reuse it any time the marker needs to move in ShowLatLong.

- We use Map.SetView to center the point that the user tapped as we set the pushpin's location.

Extra Credit: Finding Yourself on the Map

While the Bing.Maps doesn't have an API for geolocation, there is a sensor API in Windows 8 that can use WiFi geolocating or other services to obtain your location. Any Windows 8 Store application can access this API, as long as the API has "Location" enabled in the Package Manifest.

Windows 8 provides the Geolocator class in the Windows.Devices.Geolocation namepace. Using it is simple: you create one, attach event handlers to its PositionChanged and StatusChanged events, and you're all set. When you create one, the system prompts you if it's okay for the application to use the device's position; if you click "OK" to answer in the affirmative, the Geolocator instance performs a positioning operation and begins reporting your position through the PositionChanged event. If you decline the request, the Geolocator instance remains in an inactive state, and your handler receives no PositionChanged events.

One wrinkle in all of this is that the sensor system runs on a different thread than the UI thread, so the actual process of reporting your position involves a cross-thread dispatch from the PositionChanged event handler to your UI thread.

To make this all work in our sample application, we first select the Package.appxmanifest in the solution (double-click), and choose "Capabilities" (the second tab in the view that appears). Make sure that "Location" is checked, as you see in Figure 8-4.

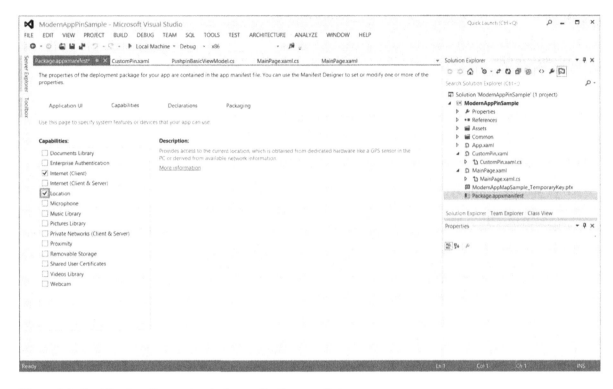

Figure 8-4. *Enabling location services in the application manifest*

Now, add using directives for the `Windows.Devices.Geolocation` and `Windows.UI.Core` to MainPage.xaml.cs. Next, edit the code-behind so that it has the fields and methods you see in Listing 8-7.

Listing 8-7. Enabling positioning in your sample application

```
CoreDispatcher mDispatcher;
Pushpin m_youAreHerePin;
Geolocator m_geolocator;
CustomPin m_pushPin;
public MainPage()
{
  this.InitializeComponent();
  VenueManager m = map.VenueManager;
  m.UseDefaultVenueTooltip = false;
  m.VenueEntityTapped += Venue_Tapped;

  mDispatcher = Dispatcher;
  Loaded += MainPage_Loaded;
}
```

```
private void MainPage_Loaded(object sender, RoutedEventArgs e)
{
  m_geolocator = new Geolocator();
  m_geolocator.PositionChanged += Geolocator_PositionChanged;
  m_geolocator.StatusChanged += Geolocator_StatusChanged;
}

private void Geolocator_StatusChanged(Geolocator g, StatusChangedEventArgs e)
{
}

private async void Geolocator_PositionChanged(Geolocator g,
                                        PositionChangedEventArgs e)
{
  await mDispatcher.RunAsync(CoreDispatcherPriority.Normal, () =>
  {
    if (m_youAreHerePin == null)
    {
      m_youAreHerePin = new Pushpin();
      map.Children.Add(m_youAreHerePin);
    }
    Location location = new Location(e.Position.Coordinate.Latitude,
      e.Position.Coordinate.Longitude);
    MapLayer.SetPosition(m_youAreHerePin, location);
  });
}
```

First, we add an event handler for the page's Loaded event, so that we only prompt the user to use location once the application UI has been fully loaded—if we instantiate a Geolocator in the page's constructor, we run the risk of showing the confirmation before the rest of the UI has drawn, which looks bad.

The event handler for the page's Loaded event creates a Geolocator instance and sets up its event handlers. Strictly speaking, we don't need a StatusChanged event handler; you can put a breakpoint there and see the state of the Geocoder change as you accept or deny the location privilege when you're prompted.

The Geolocator_PositionChanged method is an async method—this is new to C# 5.0, and makes handling multi-threaded applications ever so much simpler. When you specify a method as async, you indicate that any function call prefixed by await can run without blocking the current thread. We use await here to signal that the dispatcher's RunAsync method will its code on the UI thread, and not block this thread while that code is running. The dispatcher's RunAsync method takes a priority for the code to run and a lambda expression indicating the code to run.

Our lambda is simple: it lazily constructs a standard Pushpin instance if we don't already have one, and then places the Pushpin at the location reported by the Geolocator. Figure 8-5 shows the result of running the application at our office after clicking on Boston Commons in Boston, MA.

Figure 8-5. *A pushpin marking our office location*

Putting it All Together The Earthquake App

Figure 8-6 shows our Earthquake application reworked for Windows Store. We use a custom XAML element for our magnitude—showing pushpins, layered through a `MapItemControl` that manages our binding to our model. The detail view the application shows when you click a magnitude pin is a `Grid` in XAML in a `MapLayer` instance, so we can position it by geoposition (the position of the pin) when you click the earthquake.

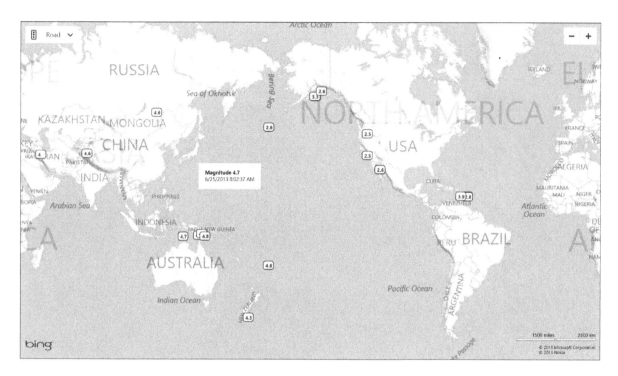

Figure 8-6. *The Earthquake App, written for Windows Store*

Listing 8-8 shows the XAML for the main page.

Listing 8-8. The application's main page XAML

```
<Page
  x:Class="ModernAppMapSample.MainPage"
  xmlns="http://schemas.microsoft.com/winfx/2006/xaml/presentation"
  xmlns:x="http://schemas.microsoft.com/winfx/2006/xaml"
  xmlns:local="using:ModernAppMapSample"
  xmlns:d=http://schemas.microsoft.com/expression/blend/2008
  xmlns:mc="http://schemas.openxmlformats.org/markup-compatibility/2006"
  xmlns:map="using:Bing.Maps"
  mc:Ignorable="d">

  <Page.Resources>
    <DataTemplate x:Key="EarthquakeTemplate">
      <local:CustomPin map:MapLayer.Position="{Binding Location}"
          Tag="{Binding}"
          Text="{Binding Magnitude}"
          Tapped="Pushpin_Tapped"/>
    </DataTemplate>
  </Page.Resources>

  <Grid Background="{StaticResource ApplicationPageBackgroundThemeBrush}">
    <map:Map Grid.Column="1"
      x:Name="map"
```

```
          Credentials="{StaticResource MyCredentials}">
        <map:Map.Children>
          <map:MapItemsControl
            ItemsSource="{Binding Earthquakes}"
            ItemTemplate="{StaticResource EarthquakeTemplate}"/>
          <map:MapLayer x:Name="ContentPopupLayer">
            <Grid
              x:Name="ContentPopup"
              Visibility="Collapsed"
              Background="White"
              Opacity="0.85">
              <StackPanel Margin="15">
                <TextBlock
                  x:Name="ContentPopupText"
                  Foreground="Black"
                  FontSize="12"
                  FontWeight="Bold"/>
                <TextBlock
                  x:Name="ContentPopupDescription"
                  Foreground="Black"
                  FontSize="12"/>
              </StackPanel>
            </Grid>
          </map:MapLayer>
        </map:Map.Children>
      </map:Map>
    </Grid>
</Page>
```

If you read Chapter 7, the XAML's strikingly similar to what you saw in Listing 7-1. We begin by specifying namespaces for the Bing Maps control (map) and the code provided by the application itself (local).

All the data binding happens with the EarthquakeTemplate data template, which uses an instance of our custom pushpin which you see in Listing 8-10 and Listing 8-11). It assumes the data model has two properties: Location, which is Bing.Maps.Location instance, and Magnitude, which is the earthquake magnitude.

The map control itself sits as the only element in the page's grid, with a child MapItemControl to handle the data binding between the model and the XAML, and ContentPopup, which is just a sub-grid with text fields for the earthquake magnitude and time of occurrence.

Listing 8-9 shows the code-behind for the main page.

Listing 8-9. The code-behind for the main page

```
public sealed partial class MainPage : Page
{
  public MainPage()
  {
    this.InitializeComponent();
    DataContext = new EarthquakeViewModel();
  }
```

```
  private void Pushpin_Tapped(object sender, TappedRoutedEventArgs e)
  {
    FrameworkElement pin = sender as FrameworkElement;
    MapLayer.SetPosition(ContentPopup, MapLayer.GetPosition(pin));

    var location = (Earthquake)pin.Tag;

    ContentPopupText.Text = "Magnitude " + location.Magnitude;
    ContentPopupDescription.Text = location.When.ToString();
    ContentPopup.Visibility = Visibility.Visible;
  }
}
```

The constructor creates our data model. The Pushpin_Tapped method shows the ContentPopup on the map layer, positioning it to the same location as the pin you tapped, and then sets the text for the popup's fields before making it visible.

Returning to the custom pushpin, we created the marker using raw XAML based on the XAML we showed in Chapter 7, although you could do something fancier in Blend. Listing 8-9 shows the XAML for the custom pushpin.

Listing 8-10. The custom pushpin XAML

```xml
<UserControl
  x:Class="ModernAppMapSample.CustomPin"
  xmlns="http://schemas.microsoft.com/winfx/2006/xaml/presentation"
  xmlns:x="http://schemas.microsoft.com/winfx/2006/xaml"
  xmlns:local="using:ModernAppMapSample"
  xmlns:d="http://schemas.microsoft.com/expression/blend/2008"
  xmlns:mc="http://schemas.openxmlformats.org/markup-compatibility/2006"
  mc:Ignorable="d"
  d:DesignWidth="400" Height="64" Width="64">

  <Grid Margin="-12,-10,0,0" Width="25" Height="20">
    <Rectangle
      Fill="White"
      RadiusX ="5"
      RadiusY="5"
      HorizontalAlignment="Left"
      VerticalAlignment="Top"
      Height="20"
      Stroke="Black"
      Width="25"
      Margin="-12,-10,0,0"/>
    <GridView
      HorizontalAlignment="Left"
      VerticalAlignment="Top"
      Height="20"
      Width="25"
      Margin="-32,-32,0,0" />
    <TextBlock x:Name="text"
      HorizontalAlignment="Left"
      VerticalAlignment="Top"
      Margin="-6,-7,0,0"
```

```
        TextWrapping="Wrap"
        Text=""
        Foreground="#FFB8000B"
        FontFamily="Segoe UI"
        FontWeight="Bold"/>
  </Grid>
</UserControl>
```

The code-behind is responsible for setting the text field in the pushpin, as you see in Listing 8-11.

Listing 8-11. The code-behind for the custom pushpin

```
public sealed partial class CustomPin : UserControl
{
  public static readonly DependencyProperty TextProperty =
    DependencyProperty.Register("Text",
      typeof(string),
      typeof(UserControl),
      new PropertyMetadata(0,
        new PropertyChangedCallback(TextPropertyChanged)));

  public string Text
  {
    get;
    set;
  }
  public CustomPin()
  {
    this.InitializeComponent();
  }

  private static void TextPropertyChanged(DependencyObject source,
    DependencyPropertyChangedEventArgs e)
  {
    var self = source as CustomPin;
    if (self != null)
    {
      self.text.Text = (string)e.NewValue;
    }
  }
}
```

The only magic here is the DependencyProperty for the text field; this and the TextPropertyChanged callback are necessary so that the pushpin correctly works with XAML's data binding and its application of the model-view-controller pattern. Callers set the text property of the pushpin, which is public. This in turn triggers a PropertyChangedCallback invoking the TextPropertyChanged method, which is responsible for actually setting the text value of the TextBlock in the XAML.

The EarthquakeModel and Earthquake classes are essentially unchanged from the previous chapter, with the exception that the Earthquake class now uses a Bing.Maps.Location instance to store the earthquake's location instead of the Microsoft.Maps.MapControl.WPF.Location class. Curious readers are directed to Listings 7-3 and 7-4, and the discussion around those listings.

Wrapping Up

The Bing Maps for Windows Store Applications SDK provides a Map class encapsulating a control that can display aerial and road imagery, as well as overlay traffic information, landmarks, and venues. The SDK includes supporting classes to encapsulate locations, venues, and landmarks.

The map control provides events for your application to handle including both internal state changes, user interaction for things like tap and double-tap events, and methods for setting the map viewport and zoom level. In addition, the SDK provides a class for enabling XAML data binding between your implementation and the rendering layer, letting you implement your application using the model-view-controller pattern. The map control can host child elements in geographic or screen space, letting you use any XAML user interface element as a marker or overlay on the map.

A feature new to this control is the ability to show venues, which typically have multiple businesses in a small space. Clicking a venue loads a venue map with additional information about the businesses in the venue, including the business names, phone numbers, and so forth.

Although the Bing Maps for Windows Store Applications SDK does not support geolocation, Windows 8 does, through the Geolocator class of the Windows.Devices.Location namespace. This class uses events to indicate the location of the device, and updates clients with the device location as it changes through events.

CHAPTER 9

■ ■ ■

Bing Maps for Windows Phone 8

Our very first experience at writing Windows Phone applications was a mapping application; in four hours we were able to visualize data from a research server on Windows Phone 7 devices running the Silverlight Bing Maps control for Windows Phone 7. If you have any experience with Microsoft technologies (we didn't!) you can easily beat our time, especially if you use the all-new control for Windows Phone 8.

In this chapter, we show you how to do just that. We show you the basic APIs for the Bing Maps control for Windows Phone as well as the Windows Phone geolocation APIs, and discuss how they're different from the interfaces you have seen in the previous chapters. We touch on the Windows Phone Toolkit, a must-have add-on that significantly increases the number of controls you can use on Windows Phone, including extending the Bing Maps interface. We close the chapter with a look at our Earthquake sample application, ported to Windows Phone 8.

Introducing Bing Maps for Windows Phone 8

Before there was Bing Maps for Windows 8 or Windows Presentation Foundation (WPF), there was the Bing Maps control for Windows Phone. With Windows Phone 7 came a Silverlight map control capable of displaying maps in symbolic or aerial view, as well as drawing the usual lines, regions, and markers. With the death of Silverlight in Windows 8, the control was rewritten from the ground up to support Windows 8.

The control itself is in the `Windows.Phone.Maps.Controls` namespace, and is named simply `Map`. As with the map control you've seen in previous chapters, there's a bevy of support classes; unlike the classes you've seen in prior chapters, they're spread across several namespaces in Windows Phone 8:

- The `GeoCoordinate` class is in `Windows.Devices.Geolocation`, where it belongs, along with the `Geolocator` class we discuss later in this chapter.

- Events raised by the map control, lines and polygons, and layers are in the `Windows.Phone.Maps.Controls` namespace.

- While you can place shapes on the map using a `MapOverlay`, the styled pushpins that match the Windows Phone experience in applications like Local Scout is part of the Windows Phone Toolkit, available from Codeplex or NuGet for all developers.

You can instantiate a Map control either in XAML or in C# in your application. In XAML, of course, you have to include the XML namespace in your XAML as part of the header declarations, like so:

```
xmlns:map="clr-namespace:Microsoft.Phone.Maps.Controls;assembly=Microsoft.Phone.Maps"
```

Then, you can simply declare a map element in the XAML's ContentPanel, like this:

```
<Grid x:Name="ContentPanel" Grid.Row="1" Margin="12,0,12,0">
  <maps:Map />
</Grid>
```

It gets even easier, though, if you use Expression Blend or the designer in Visual Studio: you can drag out a map control from the palette of controls, and it will update both the XAML header and place the Map control in the content pane.

■ **Note** When you use the designer to drag out a Map control, note that the XML markup aliases the Microsoft. Phone.Maps namespace as maps, not map. In this chapter, for consistency with the other chapters, we've continued to use the map alias, rather than Windows Phone 8's maps alias.

Of course, as with any other control, you can manually add a Map control as a child control, too; just be sure to include the leading using declaration:

```
using Microsoft.Phone.Maps.Controls;
// later, in your code after the page loads:
  Map map = new Map();
  ContentPanel.Children.Add(map);
```

The Map control has the properties you've come to expect for controlling its behavior:

- The Center property indicates the geocoordinate on which the map control is centered. (Note that the control also has Latitude and Longitude properties, but you shouldn't use those to recenter the map control; unpredictable things can happen. It's okay to read from them, though, if you just need one coordinate or the other.)

- The ZoomLevel property indicates the level of zoom for the map. Zoom levels range from 1 to 20, with higher numbers indicating greater zoom.

- You can show or hide landmarks (specific points of interest like buildings) by toggling the LandmarksEnabled property to true or false.

- You can show or hide pedestrian features of the map (things like pedestrian walkways to subway stations) by toggling the PedestrianFeaturesEnabled property to true or false.

- You can set or determine the map mode—one of symbolic roads, an aerial view, an aerial view with roads overlaid, or a terrain map with faux-relief terrain—by setting the CartographicMode property to one of Road, Aerial, Hybrid, or Terrain.

- The map control can be shown in a light-color mode or a dark-color mode; simply set the ColorMode property to one of Light or Dark. (Light is the default).

Of course, you can set all these properties in either the XAML or your C# code.

The map responds to user events to handle panning and zooming, and you can programmatically set the position of the map using various overloads of the SetView method. The control performs a little animation when you set the view, for example panning or zooming in or out. The animation serves two purposes. First, it provides the user with some context as to the source and destination of the operation. Second, it gives the map control an opportunity to load the data necessary for the rendering if it's not already cached in memory. SetView has the following overloads:

- It can take a center argument, a GeoCoordinate indicating the new center of the map.

- It can take a zoom level argument, indicating a new zoom level for the map.

- It can take a heading, indicating what compass direction should be at the top of the map. (This is handy for views where you want the map to rotate around the user as the user changes their heading.)

- It can take a pitch, an optional tilt on the map which accentuates the sense of depth a terrain map can provide.

- It can take a LocationRectangle, indicating the actual cartographic region on which to focus the map.

You can also specify an explicit animation for the view transformation, or disallow the animation altogether. (We don't recommend disallowing the animation, though, as it detracts from the fluidity of most interfaces.)

You can place lines or polygons on the map using a combination of the MapOverlay class and one or more MapPolyline or MapPolygons; typically you construct your polylines or polygons from collections of geocoordinates in your C#, create a containing MapOverlay, and then add the MapOverlay as a child. The map control combines your overlays into a MapLayer class, which lets you show and hide the overlays on your map.

The Map control generates several events, too, which you can catch programmatically. In addition to events that fire when you change a property such as pitch or heading, a Map generates the usual user events for key presses, key releases, as well as tap and hold gestures. There are also events indicating that the map has fully loaded or unloaded, as well as events indicating when the view is changing or has changed completely.

Getting Started With Bing Maps for Windows Phone 8

Before you dig in and build your first map-enabled Windows Phone 8 application, you should know three things: that the map control requires a capability in the application manifest file, how to get good-looking pushpins using the Windows Phone Toolkit, and how to set the authentication token for the map control for your application.

The Map control requires your application to have the ID_CAP_MAP capability in its application manifest. To set this:

1. Find the WMAppManifest.xml file in the solution and double-click it.

2. Choose the tab named "Capabilities".

3. Check the ID_MAP_CAP capability.

■ **Tip** Is your map-enabled Windows Phone 8 application throwing an exception when the main layout launches? Check the capabilities—you're probably missing ID_MAP_CAP.

Styled pushpins are no longer part of the baseline Windows Phone SDK, but are instead one of the many controls included in the Windows Phone Toolkit. The source code to the Windows Phone Toolkit is available on CodePlex, but by far the easiest way to install the Toolkit is through NuGet:

1. With your project solution open, choose "Manage NuGet Packages. . ." from the Projects menu.

2. Click "Online".

3. Search for "Windows Phone Toolkit".

4. Click "Install" next to the row for Windows Phone Toolkit in the center pane.

■ **Tip** Make sure you have the latest update to NuGet installed before you do this; some older versions of NuGet will fail to download the Windows Phone Toolkit with cryptic errors. To ensure you've updated NuGet, choose "Extensions and Updates. . ." from the Tools menu, click "Updates" on the left, click "Visual Studio Gallery", and see if there's an update for NuGet. If there is, install it.

The toolkit includes two classes you can use to decorate the map: the `UserLocationMarker` and the `Pushpin`. The easiest way to use either is XAML, of course; simply add the namespace for the Windows Phone toolkit to your XAML with the line

```
xmlns:toolkit="clr-namespace:Microsoft.Phone.Maps.Toolkit;assembly=Microsoft.Phone.Controls.Toolkit"
```

Once you do that, you can make either a child of your map control, like this:

```
<map:Map x:Name="map">
  <toolkit:MapExtensions.Children>
  <toolkit:Pushpin x:Name="pushpin" Content="1"/>
  </toolkit:MapExtensions.Children>
</map>
```

Of course, you can do this in your code-behind, too. Note that in either case the pushpin is a child of `MapExtensions`, not a child of the map control.

The `Pushpin` class has a `GeoCoordinate` property, which indicates the position of the pushpin, a `Content` property which lets you title the pushpin with a textual title, and generates the `Tap` event when you tap it.

The toolkit also contains a `MapItemsControl`, which you can use to data-bind a model containing positions of pushpins or other shapes to place on the map. We show you how to do this later in this chapter when we examine our Earthquake sample.

All Bing maps controls require an authentication token of some kind, so that Microsoft can track map usage across applications and meter usage appropriately. Unfortunately, the process for getting an authentication token for a Windows Phone 8 application using a map control isn't the same as it is with the Bing Maps control for the Web, WPF, or Windows 8. Annoyingly, you get the authentication token from the interface you use to submit your Windows Phone application to the Windows Phone store, and set it differently in your application, too. To obtain your token:

1. Begin the application submission process.

2. On the "Submit app" Web page, click "Map services".

3. Click "Get token".

4. You'll see an ApplicationID and an AuthenticationToken. Make a note of these.

You'll include the ApplicationID and AuthenticationToken in your application as data to assign to two properties of the `MapsSettings` class with the same names after the map control has fully loaded for the first time. To do this, you need to create an event handler for the `Loaded` event. In the event handler, assign the values to the properties like this:

```
private void myMapControl_Loaded(object sender, RoutedEventArgs e)
{
  Microsoft.Phone.Maps.MapsSettings. ApplicationContext.ApplicationId = "YourApplicationID";
  Microsoft.Phone.Maps.MapsSettings. ApplicationContext.AuthenticationToken =
  "YourAuthenticationToken";
}
```

Finding Yourself on the Map

If you read the previous chapter on Windows Store applications, you saw how to get a PC's position using the new geopositioning APIs in Windows 8. These interfaces are essentially the same on Windows Phone 8, which is further proof that Microsoft is working hard to converge these platforms to make your life easier.

At the heart of the geopositioning interface is the Geolocator class in Windows.Devices.Geolocation; this class has methods for performing single-shot location operations at varying degrees of precision as well as real-time updates of device positioning. While Windows Phone 8 does a lot of special stuff behind the scenes to conserve battery life when positioning the device, it's still your responsibility as an application developer to use this interface judiciously and only get the device's position when it's actually necessary.

To begin, your application needs the ID_CAP_LOCATION capability set; open the WMAppManifest.xml file, choose the Capabilities tab, and be sure that ID_CAP_LOCATION is set.

░ **Warning** If you create a Geolocator class instance and find it never transitions from Disabled to Enabled, check your capabilities for a missing ID_CAP_LOCATION. It's quite likely that you forgot to set it.

For most applications, a single-shot positioning request is the way to go, because it'll bring up the positioning subsystem (likely a hybrid of WiFi positioning, base station positioning, GPS, and maybe GLONASS on some of the later chipsets), get a fix to your desired degree of accuracy, and then shut the whole system down, unless there's another process already using the positioning subsystem; if so, the request piggybacks on that with virtually no added cost to battery life.

A single-shot request is easy to make, thanks to C#'s new support for asynchronous operations. Just invoke the method in Listing 9-1. When it returns, you'll have the device position.

Listing 9-1. A single-shot positioning request

```
public async Task<Windows.Devices.Geolocation.Geocoordinate>
GetSinglePositionAsync()
{
  Windows.Devices.Geolocation.Geolocator l = new
  Windows.Devices.Geolocation.Geolocator();

  Windows.Devices.Geolocation.Geoposition p =
  await geolocator.GetGeopositionAsync();

  return p.Coordinate;
}
```

This code sets up a Geolocator, and then issues a single asynchronous query using C# and WinRT's await/async pattern, so the request doesn't block the current thread while the system is handling it. When the sub-thread completes the request, it returns the resulting position.

The Geolocator has some properties you can use to fine-tune the behavior of the request. These are:

- The DesiredAccuracy property, which you can set to a relative accuracy of High or Default.

- The DesiredAccuracyInMeters property, which you can set to an uncertainty in meters.

- The ReportInterval, which indicates the minimum interval between reports if you're getting multiple position reports.

- The MovementThreshold, which is a distance in meters specifying the minimum distance the device must move before generating a new position report if you're tracking multiple positions.

If you need to track the device as it moves, you can just attach an event listener on the Geolocator's PositionChanged event, like you see in Listing 9-2.

Listing 9-2. Tracking device location every 10 seconds or when the device moves 100 meters or more

```
Geolocator m_locator;

public void positionChangedHandler(object geolocator, PositionChangedArgs args)
{
  // Extract the new position from args.Position and do something with it.
}

public void Start()
{
  if (m_locator != null) return;
  m_locator = new Geolocator;

  m_locator.ReportInterval = (uint)TimeSpan.FromSeconds(10).TotalMilliseconds; // ms
  MovementThreshold = 100; // meters

  m_locator.PositionChanged += positionChangedHandler;
}

public void Stop()
{
  m_locator.PositionChanged = null;
  m_locator = null;
}
```

Call Start to start tracking, and Stop to stop tracking. The code's pretty straightforward, and uses a cool feature of Geolocator: it tracks your position continuously as long as it has an event handler. Start creates the Geolocator, and in this example, configures it to fire a PositionChanged event every ten seconds, or anytime the device has moved more than 100 meters from its previous position. (Don't get too crazy about fine-grained positioning; noise in positioning will result in spurious positions and more battery drain if you set too fine a radius, say twenty meters or less in most cases.) Once the Geolocator is configured, the code adds the event handler to the Geolocator, and tracking begins. To stop tracking, the Stop method just removes the event handler and releases the Geolocator object.

The Geolocator class also has a second event, StatusChanged, which you can use to monitor the startup and teardown of the positioning interface, too. It happens pretty quickly, but if you want to show an annunciator as you bring up the positioning interface, add an event handler to it and test its arguments: you should see it transition from Disabled to Enabled in normal use.

Putting it All Together: The Earthquake App

Figure 9-1 shows the Earthquake application running in the Windows Phone 8 simulator. Getting this running the first time takes a bit of work; if you haven't downloaded Microsoft Visual Studio for Windows Phone 8, you'll need to do that first (Microsoft Visual Studio will prompt you to download the SDK the first time you attempt to create or open an Windows Phone 8 project), and to run the simulator, you'll need to enable virtualization in your development workstation's BIOS settings, because the simulator uses Hyper-V virtualization in order to run.

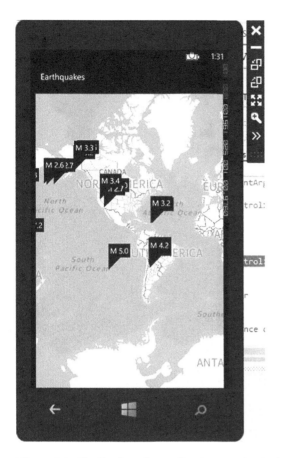

Figure 9-1. *The Earthquake application running in the Windows Phone 8 Simulator*

The user interface is a little different than the versions you saw in Chapters 7 and 8 for Windows Presentation Foundation and Windows Store, owing to the constrained screen size. We simply show pushpins with magnitudes at each earthquake location; of course, you can pan and zoom the map around to see the epicenters in more detail.

If you've studied Chapter 8 or Chapter 9's samples in any detail, most of what follows should look pretty familiar. A key difference, however, is how we handle the data binding of the model to the map control. In the initial version of the Windows 8 map control balks at dynamic data binding from the XAML, so you'll see we simply update the list used by the `MapItemsControl` when the earthquake data finishes loading on the network. The `MapItemsControl` then creates the necessary pushpins for our earthquake epicenters, and the UI is good to go.

Before we look at that in detail, let's look at the XAML for the UI, which Listing 9-3 shows. (For brevity we've elided the comments auto-generated by the new application wizard when creating a new phone application page.)

Listing 9-3. The MainPage.xaml file, defining the application title and map control

```
<phone:PhoneApplicationPage
  xmlns="http://schemas.microsoft.com/winfx/2006/xaml/presentation"
  xmlns:x="http://schemas.microsoft.com/winfx/2006/xaml"
  xmlns:phone="clr-namespace:Microsoft.Phone.Controls;assembly=Microsoft.Phone"
  xmlns:shell="clr-namespace:Microsoft.Phone.Shell;assembly=Microsoft.Phone"
  xmlns:d="http://schemas.microsoft.com/expression/blend/2008"
```

```xml
  xmlns:mc="http://schemas.openxmlformats.org/markup-compatibility/2006"
  xmlns:map="clr-namespace:Microsoft.Phone.Maps.Controls;↵
assembly=Microsoft.Phone.Maps"
  xmlns:toolkit="clr-namespace:Microsoft.Phone.Maps.Toolkit;↵
assembly=Microsoft.Phone.Controls.Toolkit"
  x:Class="PhoneApp1.MainPage"
  mc:Ignorable="d"
  FontFamily="{StaticResource PhoneFontFamilyNormal}"
  FontSize="{StaticResource PhoneFontSizeNormal}"
  Foreground="{StaticResource PhoneForegroundBrush}"
  SupportedOrientations="Portrait" Orientation="Portrait"
  shell:SystemTray.IsVisible="True">

  <!--LayoutRoot is the root grid where all page content is placed-->
  <Grid x:Name="LayoutRoot" Background="Transparent">
  <Grid.RowDefinitions>
    <RowDefinition Height="Auto"/>
    <RowDefinition Height="*"/>
  </Grid.RowDefinitions>

  <!--TitlePanel contains the name of the application and page title-->
  <StackPanel x:Name="TitlePanel"
       Grid.Row="0"
       Margin="12,17,0,28">
    <TextBlock Text="Earthquakes"
        Style="{StaticResource PhoneTextNormalStyle}"
        Margin="12,0"/>
  </StackPanel>

  <!--ContentPanel - place additional content here-->
  <Grid x:Name="ContentPanel"
      Grid.Row="1"
      Margin="12,0,12,0">
    <map:Map x:Name="map"
        Loaded="Map_Loaded">
    <toolkit:MapExtensions.Children>
      <toolkit:MapItemsControl>
      <toolkit:MapItemsControl.ItemTemplate>
        <DataTemplate>
        <toolkit:Pushpin
          GeoCoordinate="{Binding Location}"
          Content="{Binding Title}"/>
        </DataTemplate>
      </toolkit:MapItemsControl.ItemTemplate>
      </toolkit:MapItemsControl>
    </toolkit:MapExtensions.Children>
    </map:Map>
  </Grid>
  </Grid>
```

Much of this code is boilerplate; we've set in *italics* the code that we need to discuss. Working from the top:

- We add XML namespaces for the map control and the Windows Phone Toolkit: map and toolkit, respectively.

- We set the title of the application to "Earthquakes", and use only the small application title, removing the page title because our application has only one page.

- The main UI consists of the ContentPanel, which has a Map control. The Map control registers a single event handler for the Loaded event, which is implemented in the code-behind for the XAML. This event handler will transmit the application id and authentication token of our application.

- The Map control has a single child element, the Windows Phone Toolkit MapExtensions. Children element. This element contains the MapItemsControl used to contain our pushpins.

- The MapItemsControl's ItemTemplate is a toolkit Pushpin, binding the pushpin's Position to the location of the earthquake and the title of the Pushpin to the earthquake's Title string.

Listing 9-4 shows the relevant portions of the code-behind for the MainPage class.

Listing 9-4. The code-behind for the application's main page

```
using Microsoft.Phone.Maps.Toolkit;
namespace PhoneEarthquakeSample
{
  public partial class MainPage : PhoneApplicationPage
  {
    EarthquakeViewModel m_model;
    // Constructor
    public MainPage()
    {
      InitializeComponent();
      m_model = new EarthquakeViewModel(this);
    }

    private void Map_Loaded(object sender, RoutedEventArgs e)
    {
      Microsoft.Phone.Maps.MapsSettings.ApplicationContext.ApplicationId =
        "ApplicationID";
      Microsoft.Phone.Maps.MapsSettings.ApplicationContext.AuthenticationToken =
        "AuthenticationToken";
    }

    public void UpdateDataBinding()
    {
      MapExtensions.GetChildren(map).OfType<MapItemsControl>()
        .First().ItemsSource = m_model.Earthquakes;
    }
  }
}
```

The constructor creates an EarthquakeViewModel, which will automatically contact the remote service to download the earthquake data on application start. The Map control invokes the Map_Loaded method when the map is loaded to register the application's id and authentication token; in a production setting we'd replace these dummy strings with the value provided by the Windows Phone store prior to application publication.

The UpdateDataBinding is an unadulterated hack; it performs at run-time what should work at compile time, providing the model's list of earthquakes to the MapItemsControl for display. The web service client invokes this when all earthquakes have been downloaded:

```
public EarthquakeViewModel(MainPage page)
{
  USGSEarthquakeService service = new USGSEarthquakeService();
  service.GetRecentEarthquakes((o, ea) =>
    {
      Earthquakes = new ObservableCollection<Earthquake>(ea.Locations);
      page.UpdateDataBinding();
    });
}
```

Listing 9-5 shows the Earthquake class at the heart of the view model; this is unchanged from the Windows Store version of the application, which uses the System.Device.Location.GeoLocation class to store an earthquake's location.

```
using System;
using System.Collections.Generic;
using System.Linq;
using System.Text;
using System.Threading.Tasks;
using System.Device.Location;
using System.ComponentModel;

namespace PhoneEarthquakeSample
{
  public class Earthquake
  {
    public string Title { get; set; }
    public string Description { get; set; }
    public double Magnitude { get; set; }
    public GeoCoordinate Location { get; set; }
    public DateTime When { get; set; }
    public Earthquake(GeoCoordinate where, DateTime when,
                      double magnitude, string title, string description = "")
    {
      Location = where;
      When = when;
      Magnitude = magnitude;
      Title = title;
      Description = description;
    }
  }
}
```

Wrapping Up

The Bing Map control for Windows Phone 8 in the `Microsoft.Phone.Maps.Control` namespace is similar to, but not precisely the same as, the Bing Maps Control for Windows 8. You can present map data as symbolic road data, aerial views, or terrain views. You can superimpose simple shapes in XAML on the map control, or you can use geocoordinate-based polygons and polylines to mark up the map. Pushpins have been relegated to the Windows Map Toolkit, along with the `MapItemsControl` you can use to perform data binding. The authentication model for the map control is different, too; you'll need to obtain an application id and authentication token prior to publishing your application from the Windows Phone store portal. These tokens are assigned as properties of the `MapSettings` component in the map control's namespace.

■ ■ ■

CHAPTER 10

Power Map for Excel

While we both enjoy programming, we feel there's something to be said for solving a problem without needing to code: after all, no code means no bugs, right? With Power Map, a plug-in for Microsoft Excel Professional and Office 365 Professional, you can create clear geospatial visualizations of your data right from Excel. In many cases for data visualization, Power Map eliminates the need for programming altogether, letting you work directly with your data in a spreadsheet and seeing relationships right on a map. Even as a debugging tool, this can be very helpful: you can take a slice of your data from a database, import it into Excel, visualize it, and draw conclusions without needing to write code to plot data on a map.

In this chapter, we show you how to download and use Power Map, looking at our earthquake data set right from the USGS Web site. You learn how to clean up your data for presentation as charts and time series on a map of the earth, and how to customize the style of the results to meet your needs.

Introducing Power Map

For years, people have cobbled together mapping visualizations on top of Excel. A common trick was to get latitudes and longitudes of your data, and then plot data as scatter plots with the latitude on the y-axis and longitude on the y-axis, using color to differentiate different kinds of data. Still other strategies involve processing the data as much as possible in Excel and then writing a small viewer application to present just points on a map, or building a larger mapping application and embedding an Excel sheet in the application.

Power Map (formerly known as GeoFlow) from Microsoft turns all of that on its head by providing an extension to Microsoft Office Professional and Microsoft Office 365 Professional that accepts data right from Excel and plots the data on maps. Using Power Map, you can:

- Map data by latitude and longitude or geocode street address data,
- Plot magnitudes on maps as bar charts, bubbles, or heat maps,
- See how data varies over time through animations,
- Perform data aggregation such as sums or means and present the data on a map,
- Create still images and videos to embed in presentations.

Figure 10-1 shows Power Map visualizing some earthquakes from the USGS from last week.

Figure 10-1. *Power Map editing a visualization of recent earthquakes in the U.S*

Getting Power Map is easy, although the minimum requirements set a fairly high bar. You'll need Excel Professional or Office 365 Professional (the Home and Small Business SKUs don't support Power Map), along with at least 3 GB of disk space, and a gigabyte or two of RAM. As with most data visualization tasks, the bigger your data set, the more RAM you should have. You also need to ensure that you have DirectX 10 or better: the mapping visualizations make heavy use of your graphics card. Finally, while using Power Map you need to have an Internet connection, because the map data and geocoding uses Microsoft's servers as a source of data.

If you meet these requirements, head over to http://www.bit.ly/1a5xjWi and download the installer. It's the usual double-clickable installer, and may connect to the Internet to download additional libraries as it goes along.

Getting Started with Power Map

The USGS offers earthquake data in a variety of formats, and one format is a comma-separated-value (CSV) file sorted by time. Go to http://on.doi.gov/1dvKf9X and pick a file; in the example that follows we're using the file of earthquakes from the last seven days, because it's enough data to experiment with without being overwhelming.

The data has a number of fields, but the fields we'll focus on are:

- The time (which we'll need to convert to a time Excel can process for our time-series animation)

- The latitude and longitude of the earthquake event

- The magnitude of the earthquake event

- The depth of the earthquake event

Download a data set from the USGS and save it as an Excel file (you can't directly work with CSV files in Power Map, as the Power Map visualizations are saved as part of the Excel file). Before we begin our visualization, though, we need to do something about the format of the earthquake times: the times are expressed as strings in a standard format, rather than as seconds from the beginning of an epoch for Excel to process. To fix this, let's add a column "converted" in column P with a formula to convert those strings to something more useful:

1. In cell P1, enter a label like "converted date". It doesn't matter what you use here, as long as you know what it's for.

2. Select column P, right-click, and choose "Format Cells". Pick Date from the list that appears, and choose the format "3/14/12 13:30".

3. In cell P2, enter the formula

   ```
   =VALUE(MID(A2,6,2)&"/"&MID(A2,9,2)&"/"&LEFT(A2,4)&" "&
   MID(A2,12,2)&":"&MID(A2,15,2)&":"&MID(A2,18,2))
   ```

4. Copy this formula to the remaining cells of column P that have data.

The formula's simple, but a little hard to parse out. It takes the month, day, year, hour, minute, and second fields as characters of the string in cell A2, and builds a new string in month/day/year hour:minute:second format, and then passes that string to the VALUE function to get the date value for that string. The MID function takes a cell, the starting character to return, and the number of characters to return, while the LEFT function takes a cell and the number of characters on the left to return. The & operator just builds up strings; it's the string concatenation operator in Excel.

You should now be able to start Power Map by choosing "Launch Power Map" from the Power Map menu on the Insert ribbon, as you see in Figure 10-2.

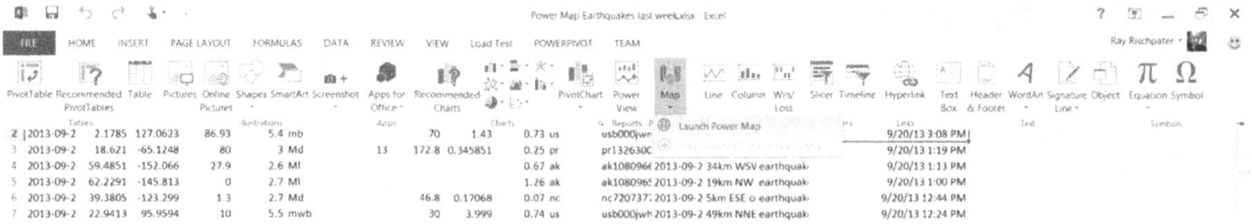

Figure 10-2. *Launching Power Map. Note our augmented data set, with USGS timestamps on the left and the computed Excel timestamps on the right*

Navigating around Power Map

Power Map lets you construct what it calls *tours* of your data: visualizations of the data in time and space. A tour is just a map with some data (possibly data over time) that the user can manipulate; you can construct multiple tours that highlight different aspects of your data.

When you launch Power Map, you'll be asked to add or open an existing tour to Power Map, and then see the main screen (Figure 10-3). It's divided up into the following sections:

- The ribbon across the top, which gives you the basic controls to Power Map.

- The visualizations present in a specific tour are in the leftmost column,

- A map (either a flat map or a globe of the earth) in the center column,

- The layer and layer properties editor in the rightmost column.

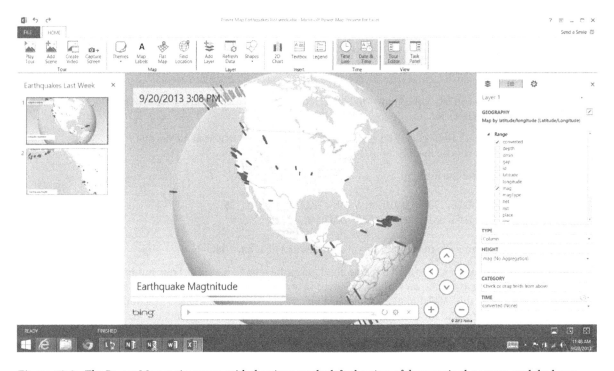

Figure 10-3. *The Power Map main screen, with the views on the left, the view of the map in the center, and the layer editor on the right*

Let's add a plot of magnitudes of our earthquakes to the tour we're creating.

1. Power Map should recognize the latitude and longitude fields in your data. If it doesn't, in the layer editor, drag them to the bottom "Geography and Map Level" box and mark them "latitude" and "longitude".

2. Click Next in the layer editor.

3. For "Type", choose "Column".

4. For "Height", drag "mag" to the Height box and choose "No Aggregation".

5. For Time, drag your converted time field label to the Time box.

You should now see something similar to Figure 10-1, with a timeline below the map of the earth. Click the play button to see an animation of earthquakes in your data set plotted over time.

Map Options in Power Map

Let's take a closer look at Figure 10-3 at the options in Power Map. On the ribbon across the top, we have the following buttons:

- "Play Tour" plays all of the open scenes of a tour, one after the other, with transitions between each tour, in the full screen.

- "Add Scene" lets you add a new scene to the tour. Scenes have layers, which we'll describe in more detail in a minute.

- "Create Video" does just that, creating a high-definition, medium-definition, or small movie for inclusion in other media (think the web or a PowerPoint presentation).

- "Themes" lets you pick a map theme. Map themes include photorealistic maps as well as symbolic maps of the world in different colors. With a theme comes default colors for the markup on the map, text legends, and the like.

- "Map Labels" shows and hides the map labels on the map.

- "Flat Map" toggles between a view of the world as a globe and a flat map using the Mercator projection.

- "Find Location" lets you enter an address (such as a street address, or a more general location such as a city or postal code), and the map will zoom in on that address. It's handy when you're trying to get a handle on how your data relates to a specific location.

- "Add Layer" lets you add an additional map layer to the scene.

- "Refresh Data" reloads the worksheet model from Excel. You'll need to do this if you go back and edit the Excel data while working in Power Map.

- "Shapes" lets you add a shape to the map.

- "2D Chart" lets you superimpose a bar chart or other graph of the ordinate you're plotting on the map in the scene. You can use it to summarize data that should both be seen spatially and summarized.

- "Textbox" lets you drop a text box over the map in the scene, where you can add additional information such as a caption to your scene.

- "Legend" lets you add a legend to your scene, which you should definitely do if your scene includes more than one layer.

- "Time Line" includes the time controller for time-series data on the map in the scene, so the user can scrub through a timeline, start and stop playback, and so forth.

- "Date & Time" toggles a label in the scene of the current date and time during time series playback.

- "Tour Editor" hides and shows the list of scenes in your tour along the left.

- "Task Panel" hides and shows the panel on the right you use for configuring a layer.

Configuring the Presentation of a Layer

Each scene in a tour lets you add one or more layers to the map. A layer is a collection of geocoded data that may vary in time. Layers have a geographic component—either a latitude and longitude or an address to locate the data point on the map in the layer—and one or more bits of data that should be plotted on the map in some way.

When creating a layer, the first thing you do is specify the geography for the layer by indicating the columns of the spreadsheet that should be parsed for position data. If your data is already geocoded, you need only indicate the latitude and longitude fields (one datum per column, please!). If your data is not geocoded, but consists of things such as addresses or city names, never fear: Power Map will geocode data, including partial data such as city and state, or just the state or country for the data. Again, you'll just select the columns of data, and indicate their type (street or city or state or country), and in plotting Power Map does the rest.

Data for a layer can be rendered in one of four ways:

- Column, which places a bar-graph style display at each geographic position for each data point,

- Bubble, which places a bubble sized to the relative size of the data at each geographic position,

- HeatMap, which renders redder colors for denser aggregations of data points,

- Region, which aggregates data by city, state, zip code or country, and colors regions based on the magnitude of the data in the region.

Which you choose isn't just a matter of choice; column presentation is best for a few discrete points, or for points widely spaced over the earth. Bubble rendering is less exact than column rendering, and a good choice when you're trying to distinguish the relative magnitude of things. Heat maps are excellent when you want to see the relative density of something: say, crime statistics or the like. And region plotting needs your data to be binned not by point but by region, so that you can visually compare distinct regions such as states against the statistic you're examining.

The value for a point can be from one column in your spreadsheet, or several. Power Map can aggregate data points into a single statistic in a variety of ways:

- By taking the sum of the statistics

- By taking the average (arithmetic mean) of the statistics

- By taking the count (not blank) or distinct count of the statistics

- By taking the minimum or maximum of the statistics

If you need a more sophisticated analysis of the data (say, is the statistic greater than the three-sigma threshold of all of your data), don't forget that you have the full power of Excel behind Power Map: just dive into Excel, make a new column, and add a formula that does what you want.

If you're plotting a time series , the time can be binned by day, month, quarter, or year, and you can present points cumulatively, so that previous data points stay on the map as new points are plotted, or only show each data point for an instant. To change this last facet of presentation, click the clock icon to the right of the Time field label, and choose either "Data shows for an instant", "Data accumulates over time", or "Data stays until it's replaced."

Styling the Power Map Result

From the ribbon, you can make gross styling changes to the map using the Themes button, or by choosing a flat map instead of a globe if that's your preference. Your choices of a map theme include some photorealistic and some symbolic maps, and some stylized maps that are best used for showing rough relationships. These themes also come with some default colors for labels; this is nice if your skills don't lend themselves to graphic design. The text boxes, legend, and the date & time labels you can apply from the legend are all movable, too, so you can position them around key parts of your map and avoid obscuring critical information.

In the task pane, the gear icon for a layer takes you to the layer options and scene options. From the layer option, you can adjust the relative size of data points being plotted (making bars higher or shorter, for example, or bubbles more or less chunky) as well as adjusting the color used to plot the data for a layer if it's appropriate (you can't change the color of heat maps or region maps). You can also choose whether Power Map presents zeros or negative data; of course, you could do that with a bit of Excel skullduggery in the data if you'd prefer.

Finally, in the scene options, you can adjust how long a scene is shown (handy if you're plotting time series) and give the scene a name. You can also control the transition from one scene to the next, using a number of transitions provided. All of this is visible when you choose "Play Tour" from the ribbon, or make a video of your tour for export to the Web or inclusion in another document.

Wrapping Up

Sometimes, all you need to do is plot your data on a map for a presentation. While you can do this using any of the Bing Maps controls you've learned about in this book, Power Map for Excel is also an option if you have Excel Professional (or Office 365 Professional) and your data fits in a spreadsheet. You can make animated presentations of data rendered as columns, heat maps, bubbles, or by region, and aggregate data, plus process the data using all of the power of Microsoft Excel.

Index

A, B

Basic binding, 50
Binary Large Objects (Blobs), 14
Bindings, 49
    basic binding, 50
    definition, 49
    IPC binding, 50
    MSMQ binding, 50
    TCP binding, 50
    web service binding, 50
Bing Map(s), 79, 101
    animated transitions, 118
    AnimationLevel values, 103
    APIs, 79
    BingMapOnAzure
        About to Map, 22
        Add Windows Azure Cloud Service Project, 24
        application on web browser, 27
        ASP.NET MVC 4 Web Application, 21
        cloud service, 25
        Map.cshtml, 23
        MVC web application, 22
        Sign In page, 25
        Website URL, 26
    bird's-eye mode, 117
    Boolean properties, 118
    building
        Map.htm, HTML code, 20
        View HTML, 19
    Children property, 119
    click handling, 107
    CredentialProvider, 102
    Earthquake App, 108
        ContentPopup, 131–132
        custom pushpin code, 133
        custom pushpin XAML, 132
        DependencyProperty, 133
        main page code, 131

        MapItemControl, 129
        Pushpin_Tapped, 132
        XAML, 130
    features, 79, 101
    geocoding, 112
        GeocodeRequest, 112
        request Credentials, 113
        SOAP service, 112
    Hello Map application, 104
    installation, 102
    Internet connection, 101
    ItineraryItem, 115
    location, 79
        findLocations function, 83
        GeoLocation model, 80
        GeoLocationProvider class, 85
        HomeController.cs model, 81
        Index() function, 81
        latitude and longitude, 80
        query location string, 80
        San Francisco and Palo Alto, location, 84
        searchRequest, 80
        user location and displays, map, 85
    Map class and properties, 118
    map control, 120
        custom Pushpin creation, 123
        enable location services, 127
        enable position, 127
        event handler, 128
        Geolocator class, 126
        Geolocator_PositionChanged, 128
        landmarks and venues, 121
        PositionChanged event, 126
        RunAsync method, 128
        SDK assembly, 120
        simple Windows Store application, 120–121
    MapCore, 103
    MapLayer, 116
    MapPolyline, 114–115

Bing Map(s) (*cont.*)
 Mode properties, 102
 modules, 79
 namespaces, 102
 obtaining account, 18
 obtaining key, 18–19
 overlays, 103
 PolygonModule, 98
 Pushpin, 103, 106
 Pushpin instances, 119
 routing (*see* Routing)
 Routing Service, 113
 SetPosition method, 119
 SetView, 118
 SetZoomLevel, 118
 TappedOverride event, 118
 theme module, 96
  add Pushpin and Infobox, 98
  loadModule() command, 96
 traffic (*see* Traffic)
 TryLocationToPixel, 118
 TryPixelToLocation, 118
 UIElement, 118
 VenueManager property, 119
 venue map, 119
 Waypoints field, 114
 Windows SDK, 102
 XAML, 101
Bing Maps API, 65
 Earthquake model, 73
  Controller, 75
  View, 75
 map view
  on Seattle location, USA, 66
  zoom level, 67
 Model-View-Controller project, 73
 polygons, 71
  around Union Square, San
   Francisco, 72
  options, 72
  zoom level, 71
 pushpin, 68
  HTML code, 69
  location set, 69–70
  option set, 70

C

Callback function, 99
Contracts, 50
 data contracts, 50
 message contracts, 50
 service contracts, 50
Crash course, WCF, 47
 client application, 61, 63
 earthquake data, 52

endpoints, 48–49
  addresses and transport scheme, 49
  bindings, 49
  contracts, 50
  example, 50
  hosting, 51
  multiple endpoints, 50–51
 service hosting, 58
 SOA and services, 47
 WCF client, 51

D

Data contracts, 50
Data visualization. *See* Power Map, Excel
Debugging, 63

E, F

Earthquake application, 140
 Earthquake class, 144
 Hyper-V virtualization, 140–141
 MainPage class, 143
 map(s), 108
  ContentPopup, 131
  custom pushpin code, 133
  custom pushpin XAML, 132
  DependencyProperty, 133
  main page code, 131
  MapItemControl, 129
  XAML, 130
 Map_Loaded method, 144
 UpdateDataBinding function, 144
 XAML file, UI, 141
Earthquake data, 52
Endpoints, 48–49
 addresses and transport scheme, 49
 bindings, 49
  basic binding, 50
  definition, 49
  TCP binding, 50
 contracts, 50
  data contracts, 50
  message contracts, 50
  service contracts, 50
 example, 50
 hosting, 51
 multiple endpoints, 50–51
Extensible Application Markup Language (XAML), 101

G

Geocoding, Bing Maps, 112
 GeocodeRequest, 112
 request Credentials, 113
 SOAP service, 112
Google Maps, 2

▓ H

Hosting, 51

▓ I, J, K

Infrastructure as a Service (IaaS), 11
IPC binding, 50

▓ L

Layer, 151
Location, 79
    findLocations function, 83
    GeoLocation model, 80
    GeoLocationProvider class, 85
    HomeController.cs model, 81
    Index() function, 81
    latitude and longitude, 80
    query location string, 80
    San Francisco and Palo Alto, location, 84
    searchRequest, 80
    user location and displays, map, 85
Location-aware applications
    Bing Maps, 2
    iOS experience, 4
    Microsoft platforms, 4
    Microsoft SQL Server, 3
    Power Maps, 4
    sample application
        architecture, 7
        Azure, 8
        client team, 9
        cloud team, 9
        content team, 9
        large-scale service, 8
        legacy service, 8
        Windows Phone application, 7
        Windows Store application, 7
        WPF version, 6
    terminology
        datum, 5
        geocode, 5
        geospatial entities, 4
        International Date Line, 5
        reverse geocode, 5
    Windows Azure, 3

▓ M, N

Mercator projection, 34
Message contracts, 50
Microsoft MapPoint, 1
MSMQ binding, 50

▓ O

Overlays, 103

▓ P, Q

Pay-per-use model, 11
Platform as a Service (PaaS), 11
PolygonModule, 98
Power Map, Excel, 147
    comma-separated-value (CSV)
        file, 148
    data fields, 148
    earthquake data visualization, 147, 149
    editing visualization, 148
    GeoFlow, 147
    Launch Power Map, 149
    layer presentation configuration, 151
        data geocoding, 151
        data point aggregation, 152
        data rendering, 152
        layer definition, 151
        layer geography
            specification, 151
        time series, 152
    map options, 150
        Add Layer, 151
        Add Scene, 150
        Create Video, 151
        Date & Time, 151
        2D Chart, 151
        Find Location, 151
        Flat Map, 151
        Legend, 151
        Map Labels, 151
        Play Tour, 150
        Refresh Data, 151
        Shapes, 151
        Task Panel, 151
        Textbox, 151
        Themes, 151
        Time Line, 151
        Tour Editor, 151
    navigation
        earthquake data
            visualization, 150
        main screen, 149–150
        tours, 149
    result styling, 152
    software and memory
        requirements, 148
    uses, 147
Power Maps, 4
Pushpin, 68, 103

R

Routing
    direction module, 89
    GeoLocation.cs model *vs.* HomeController.cs
        model, 86
    routeCallback() function, 88

S

Service contracts, 50
Software as a Service (SaaS), 11
Spatial Reference
        System (SRS), 34
SQL Database, 29
    client layer, 31
    data access, 29
        TDS, 29
        windows azure, 29
    federations, 33
    geospatial data, 34
        data insertion, 41
        geometry collections, 34
        single geometries, 34
        SRS, 34
        WKB input, 35
        WKT input, 35
    infrastructure layer, 32
    platform layer, 32
    provisioning model, 32
    service layer, 31
    setup, 36
        firewall setting
          configuration, 39
        login information, 38
        management portal, 36, 38, 40
        naming convention, 37
        SQL database creation, 36
    vs. SQL Server, 29

T, U

Tabular Data Streams (TDS), 29
TCP binding, 50
TerraServer, 1
Tours, 149
Traffic
    JSON, 95
    map.setView(), 93
    REST query, 95
    type, traffic incident, 95

V

Visual Studio Express 2012, 4

W, X, Y, Z

WCF. *See* Windows Communication Foundation (WCF)
Web service binding, 50
Well-Known Binary (WKB) input, 35
Well-Known Text (WKT) input, 35
Windows Azure
    Bing Map (*see* Bing Map(s))
    cloud computing services
        IaaS, 12
        PaaS, 12
        SaaS, 13
    data management
        Blobs, 14
        SQL databases, 15
        Tables, 14
    pay-per-use model, 11
    setting up
        account, 15–16
        90-Day Free Trial sign up page, 17
        SDK, 17–18
Windows Azure account, 15
Windows Communication Foundation (WCF), 47
    client application, 61, 63
    crash course, 47
        endpoints, 48
        SOA and services, 47
        WCF client, 51
    earthquake data, 52
    service hosting, 58
Windows Phone Bing maps, 8, 135
    asynchronous operations, 139
    C# and WinRT's await/async pattern, 139
    CartographicMode property, 136
    Center property, 136
    ColorMode property, 136
    earthquake application, 140
        Earthquake class, 144
        Hyper-V virtualization, 140–141
        MainPage class, 143
        Map_Loaded method, 144
        UpdateDataBinding function, 144
        XAML file, UI, 141
    GeoCoordinate class, 135
    Geolocator class, 139–140
    LandmarksEnabled property, 136
    MapItemsControl, 138

MapOverlay class, 137
MapsSettings class, 138
NuGet Packages, 137
PedestrianFeaturesEnabled property, 136
SetView method, 136
tracking device location, 140
UserLocationMarker, 138

Windows Phone Toolkit, 137
XML namespace, 135
ZoomLevel property, 136
Windows Presentation Foundation (WPF), 6, 135
Windows Store applications *See* Bing Map(s)
World Geodetic System of 1984 (WGS84), 34
WPF control *See* Bing Map(s)

Get the eBook for only $10!

Now you can take the weightless companion with you anywhere, anytime. Your purchase of this book entitles you to 3 electronic versions for only $10.

This Apress title will prove so indispensible that you'll want to carry it with you everywhere, which is why we are offering the eBook in **3 formats** for only $10 if you have already purchased the print book.

Convenient and fully searchable, the PDF version enables you to easily find and copy code—or perform examples by quickly toggling between instructions and applications. The MOBI format is ideal for your Kindle, while the ePUB can be utilized on a variety of mobile devices.

Go to www.apress.com/promo/tendollars to purchase your companion eBook.